Of Boys and Girls

Caleb Gattegno

Educational Solutions Worldwide Inc.

First published in the United States of America in 1975. Reprinted in 2010.

Copyright © 1975-2010 Educational Solutions Worldwide Inc.
Author: Caleb Gattegno
All rights reserved
ISBN 978-0-87825-214-5

Educational Solutions Worldwide Inc.
2nd Floor 99 University Place, New York, N.Y. 10003-4555
www.EducationalSolutions.com

Table of Contents

Preface 1

Introduction 5

1 Perception at the Service of Action 15

2 Action at the Service of Perception 25

3 Imagery, Virtually Symbolism 33

4 Finesse, Balance 43

5 Filling the World with Dynamics 53

6 Games 61

7 Drawings 77

8 Partnerships 89

9 Equity, Morality 97

10 Interest and Lack of Interest...............................107

11 Before Adolescence 119

Preface

Between the years spent entering the world and learning to cope with its many challenges, and those spent knowing oneself as power — that is, between the baby and the adolescent — all of us spend some years as boys or girls. These are the years of the elementary school. There, millions of children have been tested and tested for half a century or more, and still, I contend, they have barely been looked at.

It is strange to find that the years of the elementary school and the years of post-adolescence are the only ones which have permitted the statistical approach to reach widely accepted conclusions, a fact that does not hold for the years of early childhood and adolescence. It has seemed as if there were two plateaus in growth, two periods of steady growth or even of equilibrium, which made possible a uniform method of asking questions — verbally or otherwise — and obtaining answers which could be classified.

Perhaps in this easy way of gathering data we find the main reason why we have missed the correct meaning of childhood.

Since it was possible to accumulate numerical table upon numerical table relating to any kind of question asked about it, people who studied that age (mainly educational psychologists) believed they were making a scientific study of childhood. Only investigations presented in uniform statistical fashion were considered dignified enough to be publishable. The resulting indefinite fragmentation of the field of study provided data of an atomic character which made us lose the forest for the trees. No child had a total individual reality any more; he or she was a vague mosaic of behaviors falling between norms and deviations, lifeless and non-evolving.

Even "longitudinal" studies only led to statistical conclusions about "measurable" components. Truly the mere fact that such studies were conceived indicates that investigators were not interested in knowing childhood, only what became of people who passed through it. Their destination, as related to their performance at various ages, was all that mattered, and only the components that could be followed over the years were permitted to remain in the study. But what of the singular properties which characterize that age and are not continued in later years? They were, of course, omitted from consideration. Hence, decades of study may by design lead nowhere. Investigators were not troubled by finding so little of significance in their many years of examination of the field. They again and again asked for more time and more study, hoping to come up with so much evidence that the instruments of interpretation — such as statistics coupled with computer time — would sift the valuable from the trivial.

Unfortunately this hope does not seem to have been fulfilled — because the nature of the challenge cannot be grasped by any method of study that does not maintain its wholeness. This is why, after almost seventy-five years of study of school children, teachers are as powerless to help them grow intellectually as they were when no study was available. The studies throughout this century were like nets that could not catch fish because the mesh was unrelated to the size of the fish to be caught. The nets brought back something, indeed, but the investigators could not be sure what it was.

In this book I shall both make new proposals for the study of children of elementary school age, and provide some answers to questions I have put to myself over the years and which have helped me improve as their teacher in all the fields of study carried on in schools.

In the introduction I attempt to bridge the gap between the ages for which I have already written two monographs, published more than twenty years apart.* I am mainly concerned with maintaining the wholeness of individual life and adapting methods to suit what we study.

In a succession of chapters I shall present the construction of the functioning self that results from the acts of living that mainly show themselves in children of this age and that will in turn justify the approach we adopt in order to get the insights

---

* "The Adolescent and His Will" and "The Universe of Babies."

presented in this book. No doubt we shall see only what this light illumines, but the internal coherence of the organism at work, as well as its considerable success in solving educational problems at this age — and those depending on its achievements — will say more than the bias of this work.

With the completion of this book we have surveyed the life of human beings from conception (the baby) to the threshold of adulthood (adolescence) as a continuous unfolding of a consciousness at work on pinpointed tasks as well as on a grand design. Perhaps there will be time in this life to encompass the next two spans of adulthood and senior citizenship as they are visible to me at the end of a life of work and study of the whole, not neglecting the parts.

C. Gattegno
New York City
October 1974

Introduction

The method of work in our study of boys and girls will remain the one that served us well in the study of babies and very young children, on the one hand, and of adolescents on the other. We asked: what is there in the life of each of us that requires our full attention at a particular age, that is vital for that age or for coming ages and cannot be postponed?

We also systematically used certain principles as instruments:

- that living changes time into durable experience;
- that energy is transformed — partly in becoming new structures, new functionings — by the process we call "objectification;"
- that the order of experiencing in time must be respected — an order that cannot be reversed because one activity must follow others which condition its existence; we call this order "the temporal hierarchies;"

- that an integration process is observable — one which produces changed individuals but maintains the uniqueness and singularity of the person;

- that living in time can be equated with the use of one's past to make possible the actualizations of the present molded by the descending forms that represent the future as grasped by one's mind.

There are, of course, other instruments needed to understand this age more adequately and they will be forged as we find ourselves confronted with an actual challenge that dictates the requirement. Still, what seems necessary at the outset is that we regenerate the lighting on our study that shows growth as having three forms according to whether –

1 we consider it phenomenologically as happening now, requiring that we describe the phenomena as natural scientists do;

2 we consider it as stretching over a period of years, earning its characteristics from a multitude of functionings created in and for that growth, but remaining in one's bag * from then on; or

3 we see it as a dialectical movement within environments which are perceived with the existing instruments, but which also pressure one to take on some functionings and abandon

---

* The image of the "bag," introduced in "The Universe of Babies," conceptualizes the totality of the individual's somatic, intellectual, psychic and spiritual characteristics that constitute a self that knows itself to be separate from the environment and from other selves.

others while one is pursuing a vision of one's destiny as it appears to one's sight at that moment.

There are hundreds of millions of boys and girls at the present moment. They live in all sorts of environments. There have been billions of boys and girls in the past and there may be many more in the future. How can we hope to have a glimpse of their being, working to construct that part of the self which will serve the person who will find himself — by the sheer passage of time — beyond childhood and engaged in meeting other demands from life?

All descriptions which begin with the environment can only lead to local folklore, anecdotes and transient conclusions, which may be invalid when one wants to use the findings to understand other moments in life.

All descriptions which lump statistics together take away the only inescapable reality — that each of us is all the time the axis of his individual world and is moved by self interest — and give us meaningless averages only good for some kinds of social action. Even this action will be unjustified for some people on the basis of fact and only acceptable in a condition of powerless servitude to some historic or local dependence.

All descriptions which assimilate all of us at any age into readymade schemas — which may be fascinating to some minds unable to question the bases of the premises, and which may lead to theories that are seductive and easily acceptable, and which may even be capable of reducing some mysteries, and which may be supported by the findings of some serious investigations — are only theories nevertheless. The difficulty of understanding growth at any age is the result of a conflict between the 24–hour–a–day living that each of us contends with in his own life and the few hours that any student of any age can spare to observe a small number of examples in order to reach a truth about the total group. Statistical methods, supposed to counter this drawback, can only be trusted to deal with objects such as nails or very simple organisms.

An entirely new approach must be sought which, starting from a manageable sampling — perhaps even from one single individual, reaches an unbiased and thorough acquaintance with it, known experientially to be true by the investigator or investigators and recognized to be true for any individual outside that group in any sort of environment. Such an approach may be: What activities did I engage in at that age whose consequences are still with me, integrated and metamorphosed by my subsequent experience, but still recognizable by my self?

This yielded a remarkable crop when we applied it to babies and adolescents. Its fecundity can be tested again on boys and girls. In the case of babies we acknowledged the chunks of time that were devoted to knowing what needed to be known and, through that knowing, to educating the self, which was irreversibly changed in the process. We saw that the demands of the few weeks after birth kept in check the processing of the energy contained in lights and sounds, which only made an impact on the self after that period, beginning the sensory education of the baby. Looking in turn at the various demands of 'the need to know" we saw an organization of experience in temporal layers

Introduction

such that the latest dedication of the self to its tasks gets hold of the presence of consciousness in the already objectified forms and gives it the coloring and the tone of the present.

This extremely flexible way in which the future affects the past, because the self acts on components of its own energy manifested in the bag and sees alterations as awareness of a change within, allowed us to understand adolescence as that period of our life dedicated to knowing the self as power. Affectivity is the main concern of adolescents because at no other time is the same opportunity available. In fact, we defined adolescence by that concern and saw how a number of years are needed to provide the self with knowledge of the universe of feelings.

The years between early childhood and adolescence must not only yield their own meaning but confirm our findings for the years that precede and those that follow, where these findings are already available.

Clearly the meaning of vital experiences changes its content at ages sufficiently distant from one another, as we found both in early childhood and adolescence. At each crucial entry into a new world the vital experiences solicit the self, almost totally excluding the remainder of the universe and preventing it from affecting consciousness.

To the outsider it seems an escapist or a schizoid behavior; in fact, it is the way of working of the self in the state of concentration. Students of boys and girls have described their shortcomings with respect to the standard behavior of later ages and judged them as deficient in this or that, instead of being guided by the manifest concentration on some aspects of life and using this to learn what is vital to that age.

An example that comes to mind is the absence of interest in conservation* shown by children at some ages. Instead of being a deficiency of the mind, its absence is required by the studies in which the mind is engaged. How could "mother" be a conserved concept for a child who only meets the multitude of her appearances and must be at peace with all of them in order to count on her reality? In some areas of thinking even Piaget cannot perceive what there is to conserve because the underlying structure among the multifarious appearances escapes him! He does not yet feel these structures as vital to the performance of his jobs. Similarly there is no point in underscoring permanence when the vital tasks are only based on manifested differences.

Each life is concerned with the education of the self by the self and we must ask about each boy and girl what his or her self is doing at any moment. What is there that is being educated just at this moment through the activities engaged in? Thus, we shall respect reality and have a chance of meeting it and not just our prejudices or preconceptions.

---

* A Piagetian concept: cf., The Child's Conception of The World.

Introduction

It is easy to notice that most of us indulge in more or less the same games at more or less the same ages, that some games attract children at certain ages, but not before, and are dropped some time later.

It is easy to notice that some activities which occupy children for a while lose total appeal to most of them, as in the case of drawing, for example.

It is easy to notice that while our mind may not be stirred by some perception for a long time, the same perception becomes a strong motivation for some engagement of the self on a later occasion, as in the case of, say, money. Stressing some perceptions and ignoring others is one of the most primitive and most used functionings of the self from the time of conception. All of us use it all the time, and what is most stressed may be a guide in our study. Since stressing carries ignoring along with itself we can see why our study will be helped by knowing what is implicitly ignored, and by noticing that ignoring leaves the door open for the future to descend in the form of a new stress on what was formerly ignored.

Once a young child has explored, and made his own, the multitude of experiences which fill early childhood and go to make each five-year-old into an extremely competent user of somatic functionings (as diverse as those involved in talking, walking, seeing, hearing, etc.), there still remains the universe beyond these first Teachings which is now perceptible because those tools or instruments are at hand. All parents are struck by the physical functional changes which are visible in their children between the ages of, say, 5 and 7; in particular in the daring shown in some actions, daring which can only exist if it co-exists with increased mastery of the self over its soma and its functionings.

The age we are concerned with in this book can be called "the age of stressing action as a way of knowing," knowing oneself as well as the dynamic universe in which one finds oneself. During these years boys and girls give their universe new dimensions, construct it with their own substance and make it resemble their image. Children consume the time of their life in a two-way traffic between the self and the animated universe, ending up with dynamic mental powers as substitutes for the experience that will be offered, for new sifting and structuring, to the stressing of affectivity in adolescence.

But is there so much to find out about action that five or six years are required from each of us even though we are most efficient learning systems? The successive chapters of this book consider only a few of the activities that make action known to the self in ways that permit the multiplicity of uses that are encountered in the many different lives of men in different places and different historic times.

From the outside, an action is identified when something moves or, more generally, is made to happen. From the inside, an action is experienced when the self notices that energy has been expended and that an alteration in the perceived environment follows from it. Because the self can judge inner and outer alterations in a situation, action covers a whole spectrum of possibilities ranging from a vast expense of energy to the minutest.

While later, in adolescence and adulthood, everyone tries to discover the extent of his capacity to use as much energy as is available to the self, at the age we consider here it is the other extreme that is studied, making it the age of exploration of "finesse" and subtlety. We shall see how many of the activities of the age which involve actions are concerned with quality, rather than with magnitude, although quite a number of the actions spontaneously shift towards bringing to the fore a quantitative dimension as adolescence approaches.

The gathering of facts under the special headings of the following chapters may lead to a picture of the age that is more fragmented than the reality being looked at. It will be left to the reader to remedy a fault that the linear nature of time imposes upon verbal exposition and writing. We nevertheless hope to supply enough data to force the evocation of the past of each reader so that he or she can decide whether the study uncovers a tangible reality that will be confirmed to exist for all boys and girls who go to elementary schools all over the world.

1 Perception at the Service of Action

Each of us who has sense organs and useable muscles and a skeleton knows from within that they form an integrated whole submitted to the same will. As babies we are constantly increasing our awareness of what we can do with these gifts in our inner and in our outer environments. We know, for instance, by our expenditure of energy that we have done some work when using our body in one of many different activities: running, jumping, throwing, lifting, etc. We may know through our fatigue that we have exceeded the immediately available energy and take a rest before resuming our use of it.

Each one of us has had to study the way energy is mobilized for a certain task and to find the criteria for the amount to be mobilized so that one only entered on tasks which could be accomplished. Finding these criteria is one of the jobs done at this age in relation to the kind of challenges met in the environment.

Each one of us goes toward tasks with the totality of the self and discovers that such-and-such use of our possibilities is required to accomplish them. Because we do not know what will be asked of us we may make mistakes, either by mobilizing too much energy and being put off balance, or mobilizing too little and not getting a start.

Boys and girls are engaged in two ways in the meeting of challenges. Either they are alone and have to find out everything on their own, or they enter into a team of two or more people and obtain hints from observing the others and how they attempt to tackle, or already know how to tackle, that task. Both options being part of our lot, we all know enough examples of such solitary or group activities to be able to study how criteria for action are found. The demands of activities on each of us begin with the need to take a first step into them.

The adage which says that it is only the first step that is hard (<u>il n 'y a que le premier pas qui coûte</u>) assures us of folk awareness of the difficulty of entering into tasks. Since there are numerous tasks for children there are numerous first steps and each requires consciousness of its demands. Enough to keep them busy for some time.

Although we shall devote special chapters to the detailed study of games, which will teach us a great deal about the pinpointed demands of some activities, we shall consider a few in this chapter in order to see how each of us finds the criteria for certain actions.

1 Perception at the Service of Action

A very young child, who has so much to acquire in the field of skill in order to enter a world inhabited by people of all ages who are engaged in many activities at many different levels of performance, has to find within himself the means to make sense of what he sees in the environment. He has to learn to surrender to what he perceives, to be ready to make mistakes and to try again because he knows he does not yet know exactly what to do with himself.

This yielding to the truth of a situation, this attitude of suspended judgment, this goodwill which leads him to try even when the result is unknown or unsure, he or she does not lose when he or she ceases to be a baby or a tot and is called a boy or a girl, and we can count on the fact that he or she will continue to use it in entering on new tasks. But the accumulated learnings and the cumulative effect of learning may make some of the examined elements less visible than they were in early childhood.

Perception has been educated during almost all the time one has lived and it is already a powerful arsenal, sometimes of weapons which are immediately useable and adequate for certain tasks, sometimes barely relevant and needing the forging of new weapons to attack a new challenge, oftentimes sufficient to ensure a good start.

Action has been studied over almost the same span of time, but while perception requires an inner adaptation of the inner milieu to the inputs from the environment, action is the result of an inner initiative involving the will.

As a very young child each of us may have studied the action of throwing and discovered that energy must be directed to the hand to hold an object and to maintain it between the fingers or hands for a while until the appropriate part of the somatic structure can enter into effect with a certain expenditure of energy to guarantee a throw. The effect of the act can be perceived and noted at the same time as its relationship to the energy expended is noted. Children are engaged in this study if they are engaged in this action. They may examine whether there are properties in some objects that make some throws appear to be more effective than others. Try to throw a feather or a page of newspaper and compare it with throwing a slipper or a fork.

Very young children give a lot of time to such studies and learn a great deal from them. The act of throwing can itself become a subject of attention, resulting in improvements, but it is left for a more competent child a few years later to notice that perhaps the amount of energy required for a particular throw can be found a <u>priori</u> by some adequate "perceptive" judgment. This kind of study is made by boys and girls under specific circumstances in the game of marbles (or an equivalent throwing game) and the game of hopscotch (or an equivalent).

We study them in this chapter because they are excellent examples of how boys and girls spontaneously educate themselves thoroughly once and for all.

No child is allowed to enter the game of marbles to play with other children unless he is qualified by the level of his or her performance. Therefore, we see children stratifying themselves in teams of more or less equal competence and entering the game with a fair chance of improving themselves and winning sometimes.

Beginners at the game of marbles give themselves rules which make the challenge possible. One or more marbles are placed on a flat piece of ground, a line is drawn a certain distance from the marbles from which the players throw their own marbles, one at a time. If the distance between a stationary marble and the one just thrown is within an agreed measure (usually a span of a child's hand or foot) the thrower takes away his marble together with the one within the agreed distance. If not, he loses his marble to his opponent in the game.

Clearly the appearance is that a throw is made in a particular direction to achieve a particular distance. The rule gives a win to the player in precisely defined circumstances. But the reality is that the judgment of the thrower's eye must assess the energy to be put into the throwing apparatus to achieve a perceived end. There is a game because there is an education in it and an inner challenge to the players.

Indeed, the rules of the game and the appearance of the game are altered, according to the progress made by the players, to provide a stiffer and stiffer measure of the subordination of the judgment of the energy required for a more precise throw to the perceptual judgment of the exact location of the target found by sight. Clearly blind people cannot play marbles and if they were to play at throwing objects they would use sound as a guide.

People who can see find the game engaging precisely because its rules are molded to offer a new and more rewarding challenge every time a stage of mastery has been reached. From holding a marble between the thumb and the index finger in the beginning, players end up holding it in a cup formed of the rounded forefinger on the side and the thumb at the bottom. The marble has to be catapulted by the thumb acting as a spring, while the whole hand and the forefinger give the required orientation for a "carambol" between this marble and one of several others accumulated in a given triangle on the ground. A winner takes one or more marbles, if these are hit out of the triangle, and his own marble as well

Hence, from an easygoing, informal throw (with certain degrees of tolerance, such as bending one's body forward and winning even when a hit is not made) to a strictly erect throw with a special formation of the hand, followed by a direct hit on one or more marbles placed in a restricted space a certain distance away, we have defined an evolution of action. This entails a double movement of two activities of the mind and the soma: assessment of the quantity of energy to mobilize in specific muscles informed by the explicit judgment of one's sight that objects are at certain distances.

Naturally one also has to learn to instruct one's wrist to take and hold a certain position with respect to the arm and hand in order to obtain the needed direction for the projectile. The complex behavior is now integrated and arm, forearm, wrist, hand and thumb all work as one weapon capable of sending a projectile to a target because of all the computed operations that go to link the target to the position of the projectile. A hit represents a feedback of correct integration; otherwise, corrections at the firing line must be made to improve accuracy.

Since months of playing are needed to reach this mastery, and since one has rivals most of the time, other components accompany the game which some observers may consider to be its aim. Collecting marbles, trading coveted objects for specially-coveted marbles, fixing one's mind on the ambition to beat a certain player who seems to know how to win every time — even entertaining magic to make oneself invincible — and other components of the lasting involvement can be singled out for examination.

Without reducing the importance of these components we consider here that the game of marbles is one of the means chosen to educate children everywhere on our planet at the stage when the integration of perception with a complex activity can lead to mastery in the specific act of throwing a manageable object to secure a hit.

What has been learned in this game will be transferable through other games to different kinds of challenges. Using a rubber ball the size of a tennis ball children play at hitting others who provide a moving target by running. In baseball the hitter reverses the learning and adjusts his batting to the arriving. ball whose energy, direction and spin he must surmise and meet with sufficient concentrated energy to place it out of reach of fielders. The pitcher has a role similar to the thrower in the game of marbles and uses that training if it is available.

In archery the lessons learned in games like marbles serve to cut short the adaptation to a new form of throwing. Passing, in American or English football, again shows the transfer of a skill acquired in the game of marbles.

While boys mainly play marbles to study how perception can serve action, girls mainly prefer a game found in many parts of the world called hopscotch. (Today, perhaps, this specialization is no longer as scrupulously observed as in past decades.)

In the game of hopscotch, the players take turns at throwing a small, generally flat stone on a diagram drawn on the ground, with twigs if oh sand, with chalks if on concrete or blacktop. Various diagrams are offered to different players according to their level of mastery of the skills involved. The rules not only cover the throws, determining the order of successive placements of successful throws (with penalties in the improbable, but not infrequent, landing of the stone on a line or outside the squares), but also add difficulties by allotting players a "house" each time they complete a full turn of throwing and hopping. Each player must hop over anyone else's house in order not to be disqualified.

Clearly this additional rule distinguishes hopscotch from the game of marbles and blurs the observation that perception is serving action in this game. But because it is a game of throwing, and because each step is started with a throw, no one can take the game through a number of drawn diagrams involving harder and harder challenges unless the act of throwing is worked on and brought to a certain level of excellence. The stone is not required to hit anything, but the players have to work on their wrists, their hands and their bodies in order to determine exactly the angle of throw and the energy to be spent to secure the successive placements.

We can say in a few words that both hopscotch and the game of marbles illustrate the awareness that one's eyes do not throw, and that their coordination so as to produce a complex eye-arm-hand functioning gives sight to one's hand and control over muscular energy to one's eyes. In these two games it is perception that plays the role of guide, that serves action.

We leave for a future chapter the listing of some of the other spontaneous activities of children which could have been as useful as the games we chose to discuss here in order to show how perception serves action. la the next chapter we shall study how action serves perception.

2 Action at the Service of Perception

A consistent observation made by students of children of elementary school age is that although almost all children spontaneously get involved in drawing, almost all drop drawing as a form of expression between the ages of eight and ten.

All over the world collections of children's art have displayed a universality amid cultural differences that can only be due to a universal function found in the act of drawing. Already, in 1940, from a vast collection of drawings, I could discover the purpose of drawing for each individual. It is summed up in the title of this chapter. Indeed, "conscious" seeing is a very different mental activity from the act of seeing that results from photons reaching the retina.

Because of the spontaneous seeing that educates the brain — so that it acknowledges the quanta of energy carried by the various monochromatic photons and determines their relative intensities by totalizing the energies brought to the soma through the eye — there is a need for the self to produce the mental structures which can be used by the mind in its evocations, and to refer with certainty to the totality of the visual impact as well as to its analysis into components. Each of us spends the first few years of life in this work and later takes all this learning for granted, calling it "natural" at a later stage.

Seeing is synthetic and the self is aware of global impressions. So long as an overall impression is sufficient for the activities of living and learning in other areas, the self proposes no special exercises to itself. But because classes of impressions are being formed all the time when the light that falls on a scene changes, when the distances from which objects are seen change, when the angles from which one sees them change, the self is made aware that the analytic powers of the mind can operate through focusing, stressing and ignoring — the operations that are available from very early in life.

Any child provided with a box of colored chalks or crayons or paints can readily find a solitary game which does not need verbalization — but is compatible with it — when he discovers that color can be placed on a surface (wall, furniture, etc., as well as paper, cardboard, etc.) and places it there deliberately. The result of this activity is that an initiative of the self, known as an action because it involves the expenditure of muscular energy, leads to a perceptible creation. The result was indeed not there before the action. That particular action produced that particular result which can now strike the sight and suggest its own variations.

Actions with coloring stuffs produce perceptibly different results and new awarenesses may follow; some results are pleasing, some are not. What ways of placing colors near each other produce jarring or agreeable impacts? What effects result from the relative amount of space on a given sheet that is devoted to this or that color? Which colors merge and which give a muddy effect? What changes regularly result from mixing some colors, such as blues with yellows or reds with blues? What effects follow from surrounding some colors by others in various patterns?

All this is open to children to explore with the above tools. Not all are taken up by everybody because there are economic considerations which prevent children from getting the tools, and there are pedagogic interferences when teachers or parents do not appreciate the education that follows from this spontaneous search and force children instead to color pictures in books, or to produce patterns by folding sheets on which a few colors have been spread.

But color is only one of the opportunities for action to serve perception.

Drawings are spontaneous actions which make children practice holding a pencil so that it obeys commands from the self. This coordination of sight and muscle is certainly not the aim of children's drawing, nor its motivation. We call it rather a by-product, obtained in passing, but certainly serving all the activities that require that skill.

There have been two kinds of collections of children's drawings. Some books show a selection of drawings by one child and other books a selection of a few drawings from a number of children. *

Both kinds of collection can help in the study we are making here for they complement each other, verifying the criteria that come to the fore in each. When working with the drawings of one child (a "vertical" study) we can pursue a line of investigation for which the evidence may be lacking in a collection containing only a few drawings by any one child. On the other hand, a large number of children may produce material (a "horizontal" study) that confirms that children need to entertain similar challenges in order to acquire similar masteries. We have used both over a period of nearly forty years and found to a consistent degree that at least in the beginning drawing is used by every child to provide himself with evidence that his consciousness is involved in seeing, and in seeing more analytically. Boys and girls generally begin with the same relevant equipment. Both sexes have a body image from their prenatal experience. Both sexes have eyes which are anatomically and physiologically comparable. All are unique individuals when we consider them as endowed with a will, able to experience circumstances which are altogether unrepeatable.

On the whole there is no need constantly to be changing the topic or theme of successive drawings to undertake the job of conscious seeing. Most children find enough variety in their

---

* A third kind stems from the investigations of personality through drawing. These sometimes become test material afterwards.

outlook on one and the same source of inspiration. The most frequent themes for spontaneous drawings are human beings and houses. Indeed, to ensure that one is aware of all the components of the human figure that can be singled out we only need one generic model. And the same goes for a house.

For the human figure the body-image is the receptacle of a very complex awareness already tried out when learning, for instance, how to put something in one's mouth, or to judge which part of one's body is assailed by a mosquito or a fly. It is not the outer world that motivates drawing; we find children drawing figures so similar to the impression they make on our trained sight that we can only say that children draw themselves before they draw other people in their environment. This is possible because they do not need consciously to see proportions or shapes as outside phenomena, but to know from the mapping of their outer shield into their brain the reduced form that the self can pick up from the brain as a body image.

Children can draw with very scanty outlines a believable receptacle to endow with the awareness that it resembles something of themselves, say, their head, rendered by a closed line. Once they know that the circle they have put down divides the plane into two complementary spaces, and when they decide to draw two smaller circles to represent the eyes, they confidently and universally place them in what we recognize as the interior of the first drawing.

This choice of the inside of the circle by all children cannot result from some topological intuition of the geometrical plane, for some of them could have erroneously tried to place the eyes outside at first and then found topological criteria from their perception of faces. Children have no one they must please in this activity and are aware from inside themselves of the position of their eyes in their face as, for years, they have ordered certain voluntary muscles to contract or relax. Since their body image is a reliable instrument they use it every time it solves a problem.

Moreover, when the mouth is added .as a 'third', circle inside the outline of the head, it is never placed directly between the eyes but distinctly lower (in an oriented drawing), at least after the first drawing, if this appears unsatisfactory to the child drawing it.

Many children do not relate to their nose in the way they show they do to their eyes and mouth. Sometimes months elapse before they notice that they have left out the nose in their drawing of a face.

In fact, to indicate even more clearly that they draw in order to become more aware of their seeing, they use a device in their drawing which says, loudly," I know that this or that feature exists; I shall indicate it by including a signal telling you that I am aware of its existence, but this particular drawing aims at another particularity on which I shall work explicitly."

Hence, the content of each drawing tells two things about perception:

1 that an overall awareness of detail exists, and
2 that a special question is being investigated.

But by what it omits it also says how far the analytic seeing has yet to go to be compatible with the synthetic and to be sufficient for most activities of that age.

Since there is so much to know analytically in a face or a house, many drawings will be produced, each devoted to a particular question. And there are many different questions, which may be about position, location, relative size, texture, color, relative relationship of elements to each other, distorted or not in passing from three to two dimensions, etc. When one adds that garments are known to be separate from a figure and can be put on and taken off, their consideration by the child drawing them will result in a new set of challenges for which the action of the drawing will generate a state of certainty about his grasp of them. Not all trials present acceptable solutions to any of the above questions and there may be a number of attempts, making it clearer to investigators what a child is doing with this or that particular drawing.

When color, approval or disapproval by people in the environment, and an aesthetic feeling are added, much will be found in any drawing that can take us away from grasping its role in providing the criteria of materialization that ensure that conscious seeing has taken place.

Later, when they are taught perspective, the young draftsmen will integrate a mental attitude with their sight and prove once more that drawing is a way of knowing sight as a mental instrument of the self rather than as an organ anatomically and physiologically endowed to see everything all at once.

3 Imagery, Virtually Symbolism

We set out to find the new tasks which boys and girls, generally speaking, between the ages of five or six and ten or eleven, consider to be vital after they have given themselves to those tasks that ensure their survival in their natural and social environments.

A human environment is shot through with cultural elements that have already made demands on the youngsters we consider here — that they learn to speak a language, that they partake in the rituals and rites transmitted to them by previous generations, that they learn to accommodate to the feeding habits and the foods that are staple for their group, and so on. Children do not usually consider these matters debatable although they may in some circumstances, say, develop tastes for food which are at variance with those of their household, particularly if they can live without some foods or find alternatives. For children the boundary between the natural and the social environment is fuzzy, but growing in preciseness with time and teaching.

When we examine the ways that were open to mankind to extend its grasp of things, we find that it developed mental powers which tend to reduce the cost of action in terms of energy. These innovations were not arbitrary. Men had to respect the reality of action and to generate substitutes that could be combined with what was left of action that they did not know how to replace. For example, when the lever was proposed as a substitute for the arm in moving large rocks, its appearance and its use remained connected with those of the arm. Although there was no saving of energy as such, Man gave himself the means to tackle some tasks that had earlier been beyond him.

The power of the mind that sees a branch as a lever and an extension of an arm, is called imagination. All children demonstrate that what they became aware of during their waking hours can visit them again in their sleep through dreams that, during sleep, seem to have all the properties of reality. In our study of imagery in early childhood we noticed how the self can utilize residual mental energy in the bag to activate the functioning of sense organs cut off from the impact of the outside by the withdrawal of consciousness from it in what we call sleep, producing images which have their proper life in the active mind of the sleeper.

The tools for the production of images in the bag remain available all through life from the first few weeks after birth. Because the functioning of the sense organs is known from inside, the generation of images is everyone's birthright. But only those who become aware of it as a power of the mind will see that it can be used to amplify actions by linking an awareness of abstracted actions with actual actions.

3 Imagery, Virtually Symbolism

Before we call for the help of other hands to pull on a rope we must know that forces are additive, and we must have seen where to place people so that the resultant pull is greater than that of each person. The period of anyone's experimentation in this field is normally a great deal shorter than the time it took the inventors who had to conceive of it first. This is precisely because the gift of imagery can act upon images at a very low cost in mental energy, and through the connection of images to muscles, the correctness of a proposal can be tested virtually. The education of mankind in the use of laborsaving devices has always taken very little time once the devices were conceived, just because man's mind can acknowledge the identity of the dynamics of imagery and of actions.

The word "virtue" was originally used to express power; therefore, awareness of the power available in an action leads to an acknowledgment of what has to be done with images to produce a result that corresponds to the effect of actual action on the objects represented. It follows –

1   that we can act virtually in a way that agrees with the actual actions;

2   that we spend far less energy when we act virtually although we preserve the feeling of reality in our mind;

3   that we can give reality to the images and their dynamics and create a world in which perception is possible, although no object is present in our mind;

4   that we can acknowledge that some inner transformations of the images separate them from the real world of perception while others maintain the link. To the first we give the name "fantasy"; to the second "symbolism."

For the exploration of all this, a great deal of time is spent in spontaneous activity by children of elementary school age. While the contents of this activity will for most of them be removed during adolescence by the withdrawal and recuperation of the energy invested in it, the know-hows will remain in the form of mental dynamics available for work on any content, particularly on thought and on systems of symbols.

Speech is already available and is a very good example of virtual functioning that remains in contact with actuality. Words are neither thoughts nor symbols. They are arbitrary sounds, but they are connected in an intimate manner to meanings — that is, images or emotions or feelings, or several of these, linked to virtual actions and mental dynamics. Words are "triggers" of meanings and, hence, partake of the dynamics of the universe of the virtual.

Looking at the complex intermingling of actual actions with virtual actions that leads to what we may call semi-symbols, we can see that life at this period is concerned with vital experiences although superficially it may seem that it could do without the luxury of symbolism. In man's awareness of himself as able to extend actions to the realm of the virtual, symbolism becomes man's characteristic. Far from being a luxury, it is in it that he will find his fulfillment as man.

Boys and girls do not discuss this matter as we are doing here. They live it, and so intensely that for us to ignore this profound involvement is to miss altogether the meaning of life between 5 or 6 and 10 or 11, and, of course, what follows from this total involvement.

Toys are part of the equipment used by boys and girls to superimpose on the world of perception and actions — the true world of their age — that of extended actions, of unlimited action of a world obeying the mind.

But toys made by children, rather than ready-made, answer their inner needs better. A toy which is not structured once and for all, as a car or a doll is, is cherished more and used longer. Boys ask for more and more cars, girls for more and more dolls; but they use what I call "multivalent" toys for years, simply by acting upon them to change them into what they want. While a box can be used as a police car or an ambulance, the ready-made police car is that and only that; hence, the request for more and more cars to meet the power of the imagination of boys in contact with the unchangeable given.

While a sheet hanging on a table separates off the space underneath and turns it into the kingdom of a child where he can act out what he fancies, a furnished doll's house imposes its shape and its furniture (although it too can be used symbolically). A stick can become a horse that is ridden around the house while the tongue makes noises evocative of the sound of horses upon cobblestones. The same stick is a sword or a lance or a rifle, or even a machine gun, to be used in imaginary battles with enemies in any numbers, from any group or nation, on any soil, supplied by a fertile imagination. The TV generation has a larger supply of ready-made images and may be thought richer than the generations of children nourished on the spoken or written word. But this remains to be proved since the function of imagery can as easily transcend what has been seen as it can the more demanding verbal triggers of images. Indeed, producers of films project in their imagination what is later found in their movies.

Images are as common in our minds as words in our mouths. We live with them all day. They supply the bridge between the somatic awareness of our muscle tone and the fluidity of our thoughts which seem to float in our heads linked with the verbal apparatus and our eyes. Our awareness of images is at the same time awareness of their dynamics and of the attributes which make them handier than our working soma since we can command them to alter the world to suit our desires.

Fairies and other fantastic creatures are not alien to children nor cut off from their life. They have a well-defined place in furnishing the mind with virtually, its consistency and its logic (that of the fantastic).

To educate oneself in the use of virtuality is to let oneself go on living intimately with the images created as substitutes for actions, mentally entertaining shifts in the amounts of energy that are insufficient to provoke the muscular changes that accompany actions, but nevertheless sanctioned by the muscles that would be involved. The self recognizes this in the same way as it can prepare itself, say, for a jump, mobilizing what is needed to accomplish the action but not letting itself enter into it. The self is the judge that indeed the virtual under consideration has the same tone that would characterize the action.

In the minds of boys and girls virtual universes are put together in which the self can dwell as it pleases, dominate them, and know intimately what is possible within them.

We shall have many opportunities to illustrate the above statement from daily occurrences in the lives of elementary school boys and girls. Here we want to look more closely at the power that symbolism gives.

The extremely matter-of-fact living that goes with a total immersion in the world of action has drawn observers' attention to the appearances rather than to the invisible reality; perhaps both have been missed. The self that is in intimate contact with what goes on in the bag — day and night every hour, alerted to what is new, concentrated on accomplishing its integration, i.e., recasting the old through the effect of new awarenesses, and knowing what one has become so that one enters well-equipped into the expanded universe which opens up — this self does not miss its opportunities even though it does not attempt to share its secrets.

And we do not see that for much of this period living is a kind of dreaming, where the actual is modified by the presence of the flexible and extendable realm of the virtual.

As soon as some content of consciousness gains virtually it becomes a symbol. It becomes an instrument to conquer what needs little time and little energy but can fill the spiritual space available.

> Here I can be hero of the kind I want to be. I can transform the world by talking to my pet rabbit, can affect people's thoughts about me by forcing them to admire what I can become, and have become, instantaneously. See how I jump from building to building in pursuit of a robber, or from tall tree to tall tree to save the victim of a wild beast. Zorro and Tarzan only make visible what I have done a thousand times and confirm the realism of my dream. Cartoons exemplify for me the availability of a process which can change printed figures or symbols into a flow of mental energy that vitalizes me.

> The symbols that entertain me and that I entertain are simply those which are compatible with actions and their extensions. They may gain other meanings through the interventions of my older companions at home or at play who see new opportunities in them, such as being a "magnanimous" hero in battles, or "just" once a victory is assured, or "generous" after treasure has been rescued from pirates, and so on.

Living the dream is in no way living the unreal. On the contrary it is the way the self finds to give full humanity to itself at this age. From the moment of conception, this self knows its part in creating the real and has not yet been fooled by verbal arguments according to the laws of some restrictive logic. This self can not deny to itself that action has many possibilities, but not all; that action is the source of the awareness that virtuality exists and widens action by association with it; that virtuality is power.

If a stick can become a horse, cannot the thunder become a warning from a God who — like the sun which is everywhere and illumines most corners — is intimately mixed up with everybody's life?

Reality for man is inhabited by his many creations and every generation enters it without criteria for knowing what is man-made or God-made or Nature-made. The environment is not co-extensive with reality and each individual has his experience to testify to what is real and to what is not and makes some reconciliation between his own inner life and the life of the rest of the universe as he assumes it to be.

We are as susceptible to being taught by legends and stories as we are by facts. We carry in our bag loads of symbols knitted into the fabric of our spiritual substance. We rarely wish to be, or can be, wholly factual. We constantly use metaphors, similes and analogies to evoke meanings for others in what has meaning for us.

These are some of the dividends that come from owning a source of symbols and a capacity to renew them when we meet new circumstances. When we relate to other people's symbols we find that they grow on us, that we discover different meanings every time we yield to them, and can increase our own stock of symbols by adopting those of others. Symbols result from a functioning of the self that we call the power of symbolization.

Symbolism for each individual and symbolism for humanity not only have a different content but are two different processes. The first is alive and at work in each of us. The second is an abstraction, the sum total of all the symbolisms of individuals past and future. Because they are the symbolisms of individuals any individual has an entry into them, can assimilate some of them and make them alive for those in the next generations who care to take them from him.

Childhood is more susceptible to symbolism because it is the age that makes the machine that produces symbols through its awareness of virtuality.

4 Finesse, Balance

In the holistic view of life that we take there is no room for supremacy to be given to hereditary or to biological or to environmental factors.

Because the self dwells in its bag, which contains at the same time all that biologists, philosophers, priests, chemists, etc. have found, the self is endowed with the keys to knowing itself —

as a molecular being capable of controlling all the chemical processes that take place in the bag; as a cellular being capable of initiating all the vital processes that have taken place in the bag; as a behavior system capable of producing all the behaviors that are compatible with the soma; as a total human being capable of knowing itself as energy engaged in the previous three realms; and as free energy capable of generating new forms of being that are compatible with the pre-existing forms or of making the changes in these that permit the realization of the self. Hence, we do not hesitate to say that each individual can control his rate of physical growth and can order a stoppage of growth for some purposes and an acceleration of growth for others. The individual takes responsibility for his entry into puberty during adolescence, for example, for stopping or starting hormonic flows that affect the chemical processes that translate themselves into the stimulation of organs and the generation of new functions for these organs.

The pre-adolescents we are studying, because they know intimately that they have not finished some jobs that will involve them in the deepest awareness of the actions they can reach in their particular circumstances, issue commands through their pituitary that growth be slowed down, that ossification of the bones be kept in check, that some hormones be prevented from producing what may distract attention from the tasks at hand. Only when the self acknowledges that the danger that some unfinished job will damage the harmonious unfolding of vital functionings is over, do orders go out to release the materials held in check and make it possible for growth to be resumed on a spectrum of functions.

There is nothing mysterious in this individual control of what happens since an autonomous energy under the vigilance of a conscious self exists in the bag. Certainly no more mysterious than my capacity to write this page under the control of the self who sees to it that my thoughts are free to express themselves, subordinating to them all the mechanisms that make English available, all the muscles involved in holding the pen, in shaping the letters, the memory that supplies the spellings, the attention that retains the words until the sentences are completed, the critical mind that supervises the argument, the artist who is satisfied by the form, the thinker who is moved by the contemplated reality, the teacher who wants to be as clear as possible, the educator who wants to reach the public to affect change, the loving being who wants to remove injustices and promote a better understanding of children, the writer who wants to produce an attractive work, the dreamer who is moved by the psychological landscape he explores at this moment and is excited by it. Analytically all this is present. In fact, the synthesis of it all is a fact of life at this moment and can serve as a model for understanding how the self, at every moment in its life, sifts elements and only allows those to operate which are compatible with some project that directs all the constituent virtual and actual actions at different stages of simultaneous consciousness.

If this power is available to me now, it must also be available to everyone at every point in life.

Since it is common observation that a vast majority of children of elementary school age have a rate of physical growth smaller than before entering school and smaller than when they leave, we must enquire about the reason in terms of the overall control of the self of all that happens in its life.

This investigation is made easier if we note that at adolescence, when the individual no longer worships action, the expression of power is made through bulk, the weight, the volume of his physique.

If the self in pre-adolescence is not encumbered with additional requests from new features of its soma it can pursue in depth the acquaintances which it started in this period. Growth continues, and for different children at different rates, but at rates which do not upset the study of the self engaged in its actions.

There is certainly a great deal to learn about oneself as a system endowed with muscles and a skeleton, with inner perceptions of the ways energy can be used to affect the functioning of muscles and produce overall physical behaviors that are recognizably new and endowed with sense organs which can link one's soma more intimately with some of the attributes of the outside world.

It is during this time that we spin ourselves around our spinal axis until dizzy, that we climb trees and swing on branches, that we try to ricochet a stone on the surface of water, that we learn in no time to ride a bicycle, to skate with rollers or on ice, to slide down a banister rather than walk down the stairs, although these provoke us to climb them by twos or threes, to go up a down escalator to the annoyance of other users.

How easily motivated we were at that age to enter into games whose functions were to control the amount of energy put into effect through one's foot, giving a particular impulse to our weight that had to be shifted in one go from one square to the next on a diagram drawn on the ground! How many different games we invented when we had the use of a rope! While there is only one tug-of-war game with a rope, testing strength and endurance and played by adults as well as adolescents and children, there are a number of games with a rope which educate what we may call "finesse"

For a child who knows how to lift herself from the ground, jump rope is the opportunity to study how to delegate energy to the legs in the right amount to produce a rhythmic movement of the legs coordinated with the rhythmic movements of a rope controlled by the hands. The challenge to the arms is soon mastered and produces the framework for transferring attention to the legs and feet, although attention is returned to the hands when increased speed is required.

The game requires one to go on increasing the number of successive jumps and thus provides a feedback-count to measure the improvement resulting from practice. The game does not require the solitary player to make thousands of jumps without interruption. This component only appears when the game becomes competitive and involves a group of players and a rope manned by two people. Boxers jump rope for another purpose, as an indicator of endurance, and may well want to go on to a count of thousands of jumps.

For boys and girls, jump rope is "the" way of knowing and educating the awareness of changes of energy in relation to the functioning of the legs when jumping. Months and months are needed to ensure mastery of the dynamics. As long as mastery has not been reached, the rope is a source of excitement, of enthusiasm, and an immediate invitation to get on with the jumping.

A rope has little appeal at first unless one sees other children enjoying jumping with it and generating contagion through it. A boy or girl given a rope knows how to jump in a number of ways but is baffled by the division of attention required to turn the rope from back to front using the wrists and arms, and the concomitant commanding of the feet to lift off from the ground at the right moment just before the rope reaches the feet.

A number of mistakes in the beginning are enough for the self to know that there is plenty of time to shift attention from hands to legs, to give previously programmed orders to get both working, and then to subordinate a simple rhythm (that of the hands) to the harder one (that of the legs, since the whole body has to be lifted).

In fact, most children master this coordination on the first day. But then the question of practice — which ensures the repetition of the same succession of commands — changes itself into the exploration of what is compatible with the temporal gestalt of the one who is skipping. The initiative is the child's. He or she can speed up the rotation of the arms and at the same time order the feet to leave the ground at the swifter pace imposed by the turning rope. He or she can separate the orders given to the two feet so that they do not leave the ground together, but one after the other, although sufficiently close together to fit two movements of the legs into the time of one quick turn of the rope. He or she can try to walk while skipping and even to hop on one leg while the rope is turning.

Would it be a game if there were no successive broadening of the challenges, each proving that the previous one had been mastered and was available to be taken on to the next?

4 Finesse, Balance

When two players have one rope and decide to jump together, one of them must turn the rope, already knowing how to adjust his or her jumps to its rhythm, while the second one has to sense what is right from seeing the shoulders or eyes of the playmate go up and down and make the jumps accordingly. When a number of players take a turn in a rope game where two people are turning the rope, there is a challenge in entering and jumping at the right times rather than being caught by the flying rope and hurt.

There are modalities in this game which show that, even if the children do not express their experience as an education, and their play as hard work spent in reaching a knowing of themselves as somatic systems engaged in disciplined activities that yield specific improvements of functionings, we can say it on their behalf.

Not only are there increased challenges in the number of jumps which express good performance, in the speed of jumping which may be coupled with a large number of jumps, in changing the speed of rotation or in alternating different speeds without warning, in allowing two players to enter a turning rope from opposite directions; there are also systematic exercises to prepare for each of these which occupy the minds of the players night and day. The total immersion of the period when this game is prevalent, especially in the case of girls, feeds back to the self that the discipline is accepted, that the tasks are serious and important, that the expansion of the self which accompanies the activities, when they are well done, are all symptoms that one has refined oneself in this field. Mental indicators have been selected; their vicissitudes give information to the self which then takes the appropriate steps to cope with the increased demands; the improvements are noted by the monitoring self and a suggestion conveyed that higher sights are in order.

When the game is over for good the players have almost no memory of the sessions or the time they spent. The brand of memory built in the soma is the improved use of oneself, the availability of skillful muscular patterns stored in the mind and its imagination. The absence for most of us of anecdotal memory about the game tells us that most people do not jump rope as a social function but in order to achieve better awareness of their use of their soma. Because these games are active the gains they represent are inscribed in the ways the self manifests itself in its somatic behaviors.

Of course, the choice of games with a rope is only one among many which provide children of this age with finer uses of themselves and allow the exploration of those integrated mental-somatic actions. On a swing the younger child expects the impulse to come from outsiders; the older child discovers how to use the combination of gravitational energy — resulting from a displacement of the center of gravity with respect to the ground level — and the energy which results from a variable distribution of the masses of limbs and trunk and head within the system. Besides a gratifying feeling of independence and autonomy, the newly acquired techniques tell the child on the swing that he can give himself to the activity as long as he wants and vary as much as he wishes the height and the speed he aims at.

4 Finesse, Balance

At the same time as they study the fine characteristics of their active selves, most children deliberately conquer balance. If a boy is given a bicycle he will soon learn to ride it and begin to study whether he can ride without touching the handlebars, or with only the lightest touch of a finger. He will, one day, much later, attempt acrobatics on the bicycle, but if they require too much energy he will postpone them still later until bulk is available to him.

There seems to be a fascination in the walls that serve as guards on cliffs, bridges, promenades by the sea, quaysides, etc. Children, mainly boys, climb them and run along them to the despair of accompanying adults. Walking on imaginary or actual lines on floors or roads, putting one foot in front of the other, balancing with one's arms stretched, blindfolded or not, children of the age we are considering know precisely that they are trying to conquer parts of the world of action. A beam lying on the floor of an abandoned building seems an invitation to test oneself. A number of stepping stones scattered on the bed of a stream is another invitation to jump from one to the other while avoiding a fall.

Because it is the age of action the surrounding universe is animated by children. There seems to be a dimension to all objects that can become active and is gotten hold of by every child. Far from being the primitive alive in the child, who is seen as animistic in his outlook by some observers, it is the perceptive person who proves that he is stressing action in everything that is compatible with it. The overflow of energy at the somatic level makes him play somatic games for hours every day so that he comes to know all the expressions of the soma that we call action. He not only seems never to tire, he is at a low ebb in his somatic vulnerability. He can take endless beatings from companions and neither cry nor complain. The mere appearance of a boy of his own age seems a provocation to a physical struggle.

Intimately aware of the extent of muscle and bone resistance, he very rarely turns another's neck too far even though it is captured between his arm and forearm and against his chest. In fact, he knows, from inside, the suppleness of a body to the extent that only acrobats and fakirs do in later years.

He seems to worship action and all places where he can come in contact with it become temples sacred to him at the time.

5 Filling the World with Dynamics

When we allow ourselves to be touched by the reality of another being we find that all that pulsates in us is also present in the other. We can call this "knowing-through-love," but even people who love each other may fall into the trap of only having schemas of each other.

Knowledge of others as they actually are requires a discipline of which non-interference and total openness are the essence. In the past science could only be about generalities and therefore could not apply to knowing people in their reality, only as stereotyped abstractions.

What we are trying to do in this book is to restore to boys and girls their right to be met in their acts of living, even if this can only be done in a very limited way because the literary genre used here is that of a scientist rather than a novelist.

The boys and girls who people my mind are not only images, many of them nameless; they are myself as a boy surrounded by boys and girls of my own age brought to life by our acts of living, our gift to the moment and to the fulfillment of ourselves at that moment. What I see, in the many boys and girls in the many elementary schools where I worked, is the passionate search for truth as it appears to them in their life, the dedication to knowing the world (both inner and outer) as far as they can grasp it with their present instruments. No different, in fact, from the way I see myself in my world (inner and outer).

As a boy I was as complete as I am now many decades later. I had not accumulated the experiences of the following years but I had days as full as I now have, moments as challenging as today's, though of another kind.

In my sense of relativity I can think about my present condition and also back to that in which I found myself then. If I did not know relativity then, if I could not imagine what I would become, I could still be aware of what went on in my mind and what kind of a person I was.

This insight into myself neither reduces my chances of knowing others nor makes my life a model for all boys and girls. In fact, I developed the tools for investigating the content of everyone's childhood when I found —

1   the role of relativity in psychology from my understanding of its role in physics;

2   the meaning of evolution in psychology, being simply that we all are in time and that all phenomena are temporal;

3   the continuity of awareness, at work from conception but shifting its focus from building the vital structures in the self to their use under minimal supervision by the self;

4   that if we are all similar because we all are made of molecules, and of cells, and display common behaviors, we are nevertheless unique because our will generates out of the raw material of life a constellation of uses of our soma and psyche with a nil probability of duplication, even if we are someone's twin;

5   that it is possible to reconstruct the true course of life for anyone if I made it for myself at every period of my life by determining the temporal hierarchies available to me.

This is why I see the age of childhood as being devoted to making its world an inner dynamic entity agreeing with the outer world, visibly a function of time. I see the boy and girl as epistemologists knowing what there is to know and how to achieve that knowledge as legitimately as Locke or Hume or Kant, or anyone else among those who asked themselves, 'What is there to know?" and embarked on finding a satisfactory answer. The keen minds of boys and girls seize the fact that the world is a world in constant change. They may have heard of the static models proposed by their elders, but since nobody asks for their opinions on these matters they pursue their quest unperturbed. There is day and night, changes in the weather, the beginning and the end of many involvements, be it to take a meal or a nap. They see themselves grow and become capable of doing what was not possible earlier. They mold mud, clay or dough between their fingers and see forms change, come to life and disappear. They witness the transformation of grain to flour and to bread, or of cloth to clothes, and so on. They break things and cannot put them together.

From all this they know that the world is a place where things happen, where a few changes are reversible and many irreversible. They know that in some areas they are allowed to act and that nobody pays attention to what they do. In these areas they are as if they were in command and can compare their functionings in the outer world with those in their inner world and find some continuity, some similarity.

They have studied how twigs break, how some pieces of wood resist any pressure from them; they have studied a number of materials and learned to know them by weight, density, cohesion or viscosity, even if not one of these words is known to them. They have little interest in anything which has to remain intact, although they teach themselves to respect it in order to stay out of trouble from people capable of interfering with their peace. Whenever they can alter the environment they do it with delight, so long as it does not represent hard or routine work. Everyone can count on their cooperation if the alteration can be done easily and quickly, but will be disappointed if they expect the volunteers to be around to do the same thing spontaneously again and again.

This is because there are other things to do with one's time, more exciting things, always different for the self aware of its functionings even if, from outside, the appearance is of repetition. Indeed, a learner knows whether mastery has been reached or if there is need for further practice, and a new trial is entered upon to produce greater familiarity with the task.

What a child sees in a task is his involvement. Observers cannot reach the invisible. They have to assume it and look for evidence of its existence. Seeing a child watch cartoons on TV for five hours at a stretch may lead to a conclusion drawn from his passive presence that belies the conception of his active self. Ask him to watch documentaries or love stories for five hours and at once you will know that this special attention is for something sui generis belonging to the cartoons. Tell him that they are as uninteresting, stupid, empty and repetitive as they appear to so many grownups and he will protest, "I do not have to find them stupid because you do not like them. They are very interesting to me."

This contained activity in front of the TV set is, in fact, a proof of the capacity of children at this age to endow the slightest mention of action with the whole of themselves. It is this gift that animates their world.

We can easily live at two levels at the same time, particularly if one is virtual and the other actual. Just as we know when we shut our eyes that we can evoke what we were seeing, and know the difference between the evoked image and the seen reality because of a difference in energy content, we know that we are engaged in receiving impacts from the outer world and processing them into mental actions. Only exceptionally do some people suffer the delusion of only being concerned with one world.

Playing in a park or garden, riding a stick, jumping over a wide river which is actually a narrow path or a narrow stream, climbing a mountain while only lifting oneself onto small boulders or rocks, pursuing an entirely imaginary army in defeat — all this is ordinary currency for boys of seven or eight. It is also the way our ordinary world is made worthy of the greatest adventurer.

When a few children come together they must accommodate to each other; the younger ones let the older ones lead. The words that are spoken, the orders that are given, may be filled with different meanings by all of them, but the surrender of the younger ones and the imagination of the older ones blend to provide each with what he can accept at this moment. The older children may place a younger one as a sentry to watch for enemies that may never materialize while they climb to their fortress to prepare for battle, standing on a rock looking down on their obedient sentry and the surrounding fields. The thrill of belonging to an army that has a captain fills the soldier with pride and he holds himself erect and alert so as to be worthy of his election.

There is nothing in the world that cannot be transformed, and if Don Quixote were a child there would be nothing strange in his changing sheep into soldiers and windmills into fortresses.

Indeed, what Cervantes attributed to his hero knight is attributable to boys, without the delusion. The process is exactly the same: an attribute of the actual suffices to generate all the virtual attributes compatible with it.

Children provide themselves in this way with a dynamic universe holding in its content futures that are indeed pregnant with invisible possibilities.

Are not the visionaries in our societies operating in a similar manner, extending the appearances of reality to include what they see to be compatible with them? Is it not much easier to endow a horse with wings and let him gallop over the clouds than to solve all the problems which lead to aviation? Or to take refuge in a whale and explore the deep sea in one's mind than to produce the submarine? The sense of adventure would not be found in adults if the capacity of the minds of children to reduce obstacles through the virtual did not exist universally. The long familiarity with the virtual at this age of childhood leaves its marks on everyone, including pusillanimous and cowardly adults who can only dream acts of courage. The readiness to attempt to open doors that others have found cannot be opened owes its existence to this sense — "I can do anything" — which is only true in the virtual.

Although the movement of the mind is only in one direction, making the impossible possible, the exploration of the universe of action teaches the limitations of action and leads to a realistic attitude which nevertheless remains tinted with daring, with hope, and with incentive, that tries to break through the perceived boundaries. We gave ourselves to this education as boys and girls; we end up with a universe susceptible to change that we hope will meet our desires because we continue to see it as a universe that involves us and the workings of our minds. The boy or girl in each of us has given us a dynamic and expanding universe in which to live as spiritual beings.

6 Games

Man plays games all through life, distinguishing himself from animals who only play when young.

Games are well-defined activities determined by rules that can be verbalized or agreed to tacitly, between the player and himself when the task is of one kind, or between the players in games of another kind. Babies in their cribs play games of the first kind but as they grow older they enter into more and more contracts with partners. These contracts are mostly verbalized.

The difference between games and work as activities is sometimes blurred: most games produce gains for the players, as work does, and both are defined by the task that is entertained. But the fundamental difference between games and work is that one enters and leaves the first at definite moments, and for definite reasons, while one is generally stuck with the latter as the source of one's livelihood.

Indeed, many games perform some function in the education of the players. One enters such a game when prepared by previous exercises. Each game of this kind follows a certain evolution, generally becoming more and more demanding, and being dropped when it no longer presents challenges to the player. Other kinds of games may have a unique structure and gain their levels of difficulty through the various strengths of the players matching each other. The first kind includes most games of skill, the second includes chess, scrabble, bridge. When luck is a further component games introduce another dimension which is attractive to gamblers. Players may sometimes become spectators and learn as observers rather than as participants — for example, when taking turns in a game with other people. Spectators at public matches have a chance to gain an education by proxy.

Boys and girls play many games, mostly games of skill, but also games that explore areas of experience which will matter to them much later. We have already looked at playing marbles, at hopscotch, at games with a rope, which extend over months, or even years, and have seen the special education they provide the players.

Teachers in schools who are not original thinkers resort to using the time allocated for games to imparting experience in national public games even though these are generally only played by adults. So "games" at school gains a very restricted meaning.

In the home and in the street, in the park, or in a field, what strikes the student of games is a child's sudden interest in a certain activity and an equally sudden cessation, with, in between, a tremendous dedication to the exercises involved — perhaps to the point of spending sleep over them.

These functional games are the ones that shed light on the role of successive years in one's life. They can help observers to define the vital significance for one's education of acquiring some uses of oneself that one cannot obtain otherwise in our present world. Official education has left to these games the job of carrying out informally what perhaps it does not even suspect to be part of an individual's education. Parents, who are often baffled by the ease with which their children move from being interested in this to being interested in that, may see their offspring as unsystematic and inconsistent in their interests. Teachers who believe that schools are for the transmission of knowledge and culture from one generation to the next do not even suspect that the real education of each of us may be found in the involvement we have in evolving spontaneous games.

Believing that "children know best" how to spend their time, I have looked at games both as a player and an observer and found in the study much that was of importance for my education as educator. Restricting my attention to the games that children of this age play — which are mainly somatic in nature —. I noticed that they all have a structure in time which is imposed by the fact that a player has to be initiated into the rules, which start by being unknown and are often non-verbal; then he has to be allowed to familiarize himself with the game through practice; and finally he has to be satisfied that the skill is owned and can be used.

Playing spontaneously, apparently for fun, or learning a skill in order to earn one's living, reveal structuration of experience of the same kind. This is no accident; on the contrary it tells us that learning pervades play and must therefore appear again and again when the nature or form of the games changes. The .aim, whether earning a living or having fun, is secondary or even irrelevant to the temporal sequence that must be adopted to attain the proper use of oneself in the mastery of a functioning.

At any stage in one's evolution in life, one uses oneself to meet the unknown. Large or small questions about the unknown must be met in their character of being unknown, i.e., outside one's experience. How else could we meet the unknown than by being extremely vigilant, cautious, reflecting after each step, being alert to withdraw from a tentative involvement as soon as it proves dangerous? Although one may not look absorbed and concentrated when one is exploring the approaches to the unknown, precisely because one appears to be hesitating, concentration is high, distractions are not permitted, and mistakes are only permissible within one's vigilance.

Again and again every learner at any age sees that during this phase much time is needed for little visible progress. But the feeling that some aspect of the unknown is becoming more familiar, that one's self has passed from not knowing what to do to being engaged in an action that yields at least something, that is not an expected blunder, feeds back to the self that the process of learning is on the move. This generates confidence and the will to pursue the activity. Persistence at this stage can also stem from a comparison of oneself with more advanced players who show clearly that there are other levels of performance than the one one is witnessing in one's own case.

The first phase may last for minutes or for days. In the case of learning to ride a bicycle, for instance, there are several components to become aware of and to coordinate before one feels comfortable that one is on the saddle and ready to go. It may take many trials if one has to do it all alone, but only a few minutes if someone can supply the verticality of the bicycle and the first push or even the equilibrium of the rider-bicycle system. In the case of learning to jump a rope, where all must be done by oneself, it may take many many trials just to know how to start jumping. In the case of games of marbles the phase of learning to hold the marble on one's thumb to push it in a given direction, although not a first requirement, takes quite some time.

It is clear that within a game that has many ramifications and takes a long time to be covered there are many "first" phases — all the stages when a new skill is suddenly added.

The first phase — which can be called "contact with the unknown" — testifies to the adventurousness of man and his readiness to throw himself into uncharted activities. It also testifies to the difference between seeing a display of activity and producing that display oneself. In the first phase the ignorance of the player translates itself into clumsiness, into awareness that this clumsiness is not a final indication of potential but only of one's present state of ignorance which will recede when one has inner criteria and can change the behavior. Looking at others and guessing how to command certain uses of oneself so as to produce with one's system what one imagines will resemble what one sees, is often mistakenly called imitation and said to be the way of learning the field of a new skill. But this complex procedure involves mental processes that we can call "transformations," since eyes see and muscles act and the will to act on the muscles must be illumined by intelligence of the process. Phase one is the hardest precisely because that intelligence cannot be trusted yet. The cautious attitude of beginners in any field comes from these uncertainties.

Caution does not mean lack of courage. Only that we are confronting the unknown. In fact, not all games are dangerous, and fears do not automatically accompany the entrance into a new game. But caution is always required by lack of knowledge, at least in those cases where hidden elements are needed to start the game.

We spoke of intelligence in the context of entering a game. There is no doubt that we are using our somatic intelligence when we trust that we know how to translate what we see into what we should do. It is much more than the nervous reflex act when a stimulus generates a response. The caution shown by the players entering a game excludes such a simple model. Instead it tells us that the self is aware of its lack of knowledge but is prepared to take a risk in formulating some somatic behavior and test it against the self's image of the demands, or of what other people do. The workings of the self in this beginning phase can become visible only to the new player, and then only if he is interested to know what goes on as well as in succeeding. Successful players often know very little of their functionings and do not make the link between play and learning.

Nevertheless the teachings of phase one cannot be learned at any other moment. Attention to it provides insight into many human functionings which may look very mysterious, and can serve us well in making us into better teachers.

It tells us that we use these moments to throw bridges between parts of our brain that have been educated to process some special information by earlier exercises, but which are not functionally connected, and that with these bridges we can use more of ourselves since we may now have two sets of signals capable of triggering the same behavior.

It tells us that our brain only works when it has been educated — that is, when it has been especially activated by the self to enter into specific apprehensions of the sources of impacts upon the soma, impacts that only gain their meaning because awareness dwells in them. It tells us that the self knows the brain from the inside much better than neuro- surgeons know it from the outside, for the self knows where to go to find available clusters of cells to dedicate to a new behavior, and what to do to make these cells sensitive to an impact which has now been isolated and how to make the newly-launched functioning benefit through association with parts of the brain already educated, thus increasing the yields of the parts while increasing the powers of the whole. As an instrument of the self, the brain, specifically called in to provide the somatic basis of the apprenticeship, can now become the affected part that proves that the self has given itself the equivalent of the time that had to be spent in finding how to recognize the new challenge and how to respond to it. In that part of the brain are placed the automatic loops which can instantly respond with massive recognition and adequate energy to specific demands of the perceptive system — which has also been educated in new recognitions.

Phase two of the apprenticeship is devoted to the establishment of criteria for the various recognitions. This phase is characterized by what we call practice. In fact, it is a period of extension of awareness so that one can alter what already exists to make it accommodate to the demands of the new.

When the self perceives that time must be given to making a functioning smoother, more accurate, swifter, it provides more cells in the brain that are at the disposal of the images formed through perception, giving them a place among all previous images, but it also recasts their connections so that a whole set of superimposed circuits of neurons can receive impacts that are recognizable in various degrees of subordination. Not only are specific neurons brought in to be affected by awarenesses that were not operating earlier, but these neurons, which were already linked to each other for specific responses, can now benefit from the accumulated work done by gaining a hold on the triggers which mobilize them.

Gaining such dominance over previous somatic brain organizations leads to a more efficient use of the existing functionings and to a sense of power released by the new possibility of what was impossible before. The elation accompanying a movement towards mastery is always visible in players who have done well; it also indicates that the self has found what it needs to turn a project into a reality.

The soma changes as a result of all this, although appearances may not change at all. For indeed, the soma "is" its functionings as well as its structures. A self with the capacity to skip or hop is not the same as a self without this capacity. Every boy or girl knows this and aims to become more himself or herself by devoting time — the substance of life — to this transformation.

Children neither need persuasion to enter some games, nor urging to persist for hours through demanding exercises. The feedback is an inner one even when an appreciative audience applauds. The inner subtle recognition that a change here or a change there is just what is needed to free a functioning, or to bring in a needed contribution from stored know-hows, keeps the self at work on the components of this field of activity. All this, though invisible to the optical eye, is recognizable by the insight that is activated by feedbacks in the self.

Phase two shows swifter involvements, more complex behaviors, longer stretches of practice, a progressive shifting from concentration on the thing one has to integrate to being the transformed person who has integrated it. The speed of change from one kind of involvement to another, though it proves greater acquaintance with the field which one is working in, may baffle observers who have no time to notice the mechanism of the cumulative effect of learning. Every one of us has access to the luxury of all the details of any apprenticeship provided he himself is the apprentice. This access seems closed by the swiftness of movement of an invisible self acting through invisible functionings upon barely visible material stuff.

In learning to ride a bicycle one may fall, get up at once, remount, go a little further, fall again, get up once more, put oneself on the saddle again, somehow manage to ride much further before falling again, and soon have all this behind one, even forgotten, moving instead towards using the mastery attained to conquer new worlds.

It has not been possible to study phase two without finding phase three surreptitiously showing its head. Indeed, two kinds of mastery are involved: mastery which sets the seal of achievement on the whole of the new functioning, which is the characteristics of phase three, and the "local" masteries which tell the self that in this or that particular functioning the required state of smoothness or integration has been achieved and that it can get on with a different task in the whole complex.

This subtle mixture of the perceptions of local and total mastery is replaced by a clear perception that mastery has been achieved, i.e., phase four, when the self utilizes the gains made to move to an altogether different involvement.

The hierarchy of games played by boys and girls illustrates this fact. Once all the functionings that result from playing marbles for some time are available to the self, new challenges are perceived. Can we be as good at hitting a moving object as we were a static target? A soft ball and running playmates are now required and the game looks very different from the one that preceded it — more so when cunning runners deceive the hitter by turning, running up and down the terrain, hiding behind trees, and so on.

A bow and arrow, a target that can be placed as near or as far away as one likes, that is as narrow or as wide as one chooses; perhaps the proximity of a hit known to the shooter only through the sounds of a voice calling or a gong being hit, the shooter being blindfolded — all these increasingly difficult challenges suggest the use of the self and its temporal hierarchies set in the brain by the educations that previous games have provided.

It is possible that, instead of refining the self so as to create new functionings to take man further on the road to using himself with greater mastery, when imagination enters, the target can occupy the mind. Then instead of games we may have wars, and weapons industries which increase the probability of reaching a target by putting a machine gun at the disposal of the soldier instead of a gun, which has already replaced the bow and arrow. A gun still retains something which reminds us of the role of the self in finding its target and shooting at it. The machine gun works on the probabilities of hits and increases its chances only by increasing the number of throws to saturation levels.

The only fun a machine gun offers boys and girls is the noise it makes and the feeling of power that goes with the domination of a situation.

Boys and girls play all sorts of games — from dice and card games that only require one, two or three players to team games, such as football, that need many. Because games are the way the self gives itself a spontaneous education, all games which reveal a reachable aspect of the self can be entered into. Of course, no game will be played for long if it only repeats a previous game under another guise.

If chance is an element that catches the interest, then games of chance will be acceptable. But if certainty rather than probability is what needs to be studied, games of chance will be postponed.

If knowing a person is of interest then any game that that person wants to play (including games of chance) will be acceptable.

If learning to be a loser is important then one enters into games where there are winners and losers to offer oneself an opportunity to contemplate the effects of losing.

If learning to be a leader is significant then one gets involved in actions which give one the chance to select partners, to organize them within the rules of team operation, and to give oneself the right to change things as one learns by experience. Such games can be invented for the purpose.

If learning about strategy is of interest then activities which offer the opportunity to spend time contemplating it become worthwhile and one enters into them and pursues them.

If learning about one's imagination or one's creative mental powers becomes important then specific games that foster these powers become attractive.

Games of chance are examples that tell us that the world of boys and girls is ruled by their own structurations. They can intervene in their universe by changing the course of things, and in games of chance they are proved, when they lose, and particularly when they lose a number of times in succession, to be doomed, to have invisible forces which are capricious and untraceable at work against them. For a long while games of chance bring out the worst in them, manifested by bad moods and a willingness to spoil the game by leaving it. Later on, vaguely reconciled to the unpredictability of chance, they try to cajole it or to use magic (it seems to be of the same nature) to turn it in their favor. They feel no particular mental discomfort that chance must abandon others to be on their side. Much, much later in life games of chance can be seen for what they are and the decision to remain in or drop out of the game based on an estimation of the odds.

If there is more than one child in a family, and the age difference not more than three or four years, many games serve the purpose of increasing the acquaintance between the siblings. The opportunity of being together for a stretch of time, involved in apparently the same activity, giving and receiving orders, testing one's imagination against that of the other, one's tolerance of the other, one's cruelty, resistance to being teased, capacity to tease, capacity to restrain oneself, to control one's tears, to refrain from calling on adult assistance against the other, and so on, are also motivations for entering into some games. A great deal of psychology is learned, a great deal about oneself, one's responsiveness to others, one's ability to manipulate, lead, engage, entertain, and so on. The memory of some of these moments lingers and enhances their significance as educators of the social being in each of us.

In games there are no failures for mistakes are permissible and penalties remove the sense of guilt. One always learns, perhaps more from mistakes than from straight hits. An awareness of the positive role of mistakes and the value of being confronted with the results of one's actions, whatever they are, is part of the education derived from games. The loser in a game of chance cannot see any mistake in his actions yet finds that failure exists. It must be placed on someone else's shoulders since it was caused not by his own actions but by a mysterious and unfair force just when he expected to do well.

Failure results from irrationality, not from the activity. Games in which one can learn to know oneself as a loser are then considered as acceptable activities to engage in — although no doubt one prefers to be blessed and to be proved so by winning. Assimilation of the failure to be chosen to a mysterious force can be seen as failure of oneself and a source of a distorted view of oneself. Games where there is a winner and one or more losers provide an opportunity to gain an education aside from the activity that forms the content of the game: education through the addition of a mood associated with the outcome of the game — triumphant if winning, sad and perplexed if one has lost. A multitude of games have adversaries, rivals and opponents, forming the teams at play. They make it plain that "we can't win them all" and provide the basis for a view of oneself as a competitor exerting himself to be the winner or to make the other the loser.

Sometimes adversary games lead to the recognition of one's mastery in some use of oneself or of this mastery in another, nourishing a pride in oneself or admiration for the other. These are by-products of the activity.

In games involving many players in two teams, each will need a leader. Boys and girls may value the game as much for the opportunity it gives them to learn to lead, and to assess the qualities required by the activity in others, as for the activity itself. Sometimes to be the leader on a school ground one needs only to be there first for one's claim to that space at that time for a particular game to be accepted. As the players arrive, their distribution into the two teams is made by one of many methods of choice: "eeny, meeny, miny, mo," for example, or the captains walking towards each other, foot in front of foot, until one treads on the other. Soon a "half foot" (a foot placed transversally across the line) or even a "quarter foot" (the tip of a shoe crossing the line) are admissible to give the right to choose first. A leader, a captain, takes part in the ritual of selection as seriously as in the rest of the game to which it soon belongs. All these devices indicate a shift from the purely content-filled game to a mixed game where social challenges are noted, extracted and dealt with. Getting into a team can become as much a preoccupation as being a wise leader, selecting the fit, the strong, and the swift to be on one's side to give oneself a better chance to win. Children feel unfairnesses as horrible acts and if two teams are selected that result in an enormous advantage for one side, the game is neither worth playing nor watching. Two teams that have an equal chance to win are the only acceptable match.

This will not prevent children from giving their enthusiastic allegiance to an adult team that plays to win, i.e., to make others lose. This is a different affair. Both kinds affect one, but the adulated team operates on an inaccessible plane, whereas the vital games one engages in serve one's growth as well as that of the other players.

Games are of paramount importance in our lives and when we are boys and girls they form the most significant part of our days. They are the source of our true education, the one that will remain with us in the form of a multitude of smooth functionings, of an arsenal of enhanced sensitivities leading to deeper and clearer perceptions. They are also the vehicles for additional lessons about ourselves and our human and natural environment.

Much has been left unreported here. Discovering and collating what will become the folklore of the ways of knowing oneself through games must wait for more perceptive observers of boys and girls.

7 Drawings

In the previous chapter we returned to a study begun in Chapter 1 and found that much more was available in the field. In this chapter we shall pursue what we started in Chapter 2, and again find that the instruments we are using are capable of adding much to our insights into the workings of the mind. Once again we can call our study psychological or human according to whether we consider only the individual or take ourselves as specimens of humanity.

We reiterate that since our eyes are specialized instruments of the mind they change by the mere fact that they are given opportunities to enter into new fields and perform new functions. The baby has already gained new powers that the anatomy and physiology of the organs permit but which are of another nature.

That we know what we know, in terms of our sight, has already been used to generate labels for colors, hues, shades, shapes, spatial relations and particular attributes such as sex, orderliness, etc., all of which are perceptible through the eye.

This shows how the eye as an instrument of the mind has organized the environment into categories which ease the ways we can handle it mentally, allowing images to replace reality.

Awareness that images are close to reality, though distinct from it, comes from simple exercises like shutting one's eyes, or recalling a past event, or from dreams that linger after we wake up.

Awareness that images have at their disposal the dynamics of the mind comes from the ease with which we can evoke two of them and mingle them — putting, for example, a human head and torso onto the body of a horse, or wings onto another horse.

Awareness of reality through the added energy that is actually received by the soma normally keeps us from totally replacing the virtual by the actual, and conversely. This is our birthright — as it is that of any creature endowed with sensors that can be affected by outside energy as well as activated from the inside.

In man's case the contact — through awareness of the self — with all and every energized element in the bag does not permit him to confuse images and reality but it permits him to entertain a study of reality through studying images which have a power that is not shared by reality: that they can be reached when he is asleep. So the self gives itself the task of preparing to live nearer to reality by ensuring that images be as well known as reality can be known. Much of dreaming, which does not involve emotions but nevertheless goes on for hours in sleep, is concerned with this study of the meaning of images made during the waking state.

When we wake up and know that the energy from photons or noises is added to our system we can not only transfer our tools to the study of what we are seeing or hearing but can discover discrepancies between what we became aware of in our sleep and what we are now noticing. This awareness of discrepancy motivates us consciously to look closer at reality and to focus on what we may have missed and found lacking in the image.

A series of drawings by any one boy or girl will tell us that those that follow waking are connected with those of the previous period of drawing, showing a continuity of investigation concerned with a need to know more about some very precise element.

When the evidence is gathered it becomes clear that our life is a continuum of inner activity in which the relation of the self to reality produces reliable substitutes for it in the bag that can be handled more easily and more adequately in sleep, thus preparing for a further encounter with the "total reality" in the waking state, and so on. Drawings being halfway between the image and reality, serve as feedback mechanisms. But they also reveal in a unique way what the mind of the producer of the drawing is working on.

Between perception and conscious perception there is the difference that from the infinity of components capable of reaching the bag and together making an impact on it, some elements are stressed for some purpose through an enhancement of the sensitivity of particular receptors while the rest are denied access and can be considered to be ignored. Thus, conscious perception is recognizable by this deliberate movement of energy and can be called concentration, or focusing on that which is stressed. The rest does not disappear, it is simply ignored or not stressed.

Man has invented drawing as a testimony to the evolution of his conscious perception and each drawing tells a story in this respect. It can tell other stories to observers who necessarily have a different viewpoint and look at the final product as a whole, finding loveliness, beauty, originality and a thousand other attributes in it. But for the boys and girls who produce the drawings, all these attributes are secondary, anecdotal in character, and no drawing is so precious that it must be preserved.

Placed in the larger context of having a vital function to perform, children's drawings can serve as an instrument for the understanding of what we do with ourselves at a particular stage in our life. If we go on spontaneously drawing for about four years between the ages of five and ten and suddenly give up the activity — unless we take it up as an expression of our whole self and become artists — are we not saying that drawing, like playing certain games is a way of knowing? Of knowing what it is to see? It is a way of knowing which speaks of a double movement: how we are affected by what we know as reality, and how reality is constructed in each of us. Reality (with a big R) is at the same time an assumption, an idea, and a guide that remains suspended in our judgment, never totally known, never needing to be known, but a convenient frame of reference accommodating to the studies of all men, uniting those who reach what they can acknowledge to be the same conclusion, justifying those who differ and keeping the future open while making the past understandable. The assumption is convenient for a boy or girl as well as for the philosopher; he or she returns to it and sees more of it, receives more from it.

In order to follow this epistemological career the child who works on reality in order to construct his reality — the one that will permit him to dream as well as be at peace with events in his environment — draws as well as plays. His drawings are in space and his games in time. The former, though each is considered as a moment in a study, are more permanent than the latter, which can be seen and lived on the abstract canvas of duration and which can last for weeks or even months.

We need a large collection of drawings to ascertain that a child is undertaking particular studies and delving more deeply into the investigation he is entertaining. Fortunately young artists are prolific and there is no dearth of large collections. The points I have made above are so clearly illustrated in the collections I gathered that I find it hard to believe that so few observers have discovered them. Is this because the wealth of the drawings can be used to illustrate so many different viewpoints that observers can take? I prefer to believe this than that the obvious has escaped so many.

Let us consciously look at a face and make a list of what is present there that may require numerous successive drawings by one child who is working on knowing what it is to see all that a face shows.

We can first list the items that one immediately acknowledges as distinct: the face as surface, a boundary between the world and that part of the bag; the two eyes; one nose and two nostrils; one mouth; two ears; a brow; two eyebrows; hair.

Then we note the details of each item: the eyes have eyelids, eyelashes, a pupil, a white part, lacrimal glands; the mouth has lips, teeth; the face has cheeks, a chin, temples, a lower jaw; ears have lobes, convolutions, a rim; a nose has relief, two contours for the nostrils; hair sits on and surrounds the face. Then we see how the placing of each item in the whole requires awareness of relative position and of relative and absolute size.

Finally there are invisible elements which generate the awareness of relationships, of the blending of the parts, of the resemblance to a human face which may carry any one of the many expressions of emotion, mood or posture.

Clearly to investigate all this requires much to be done, and since there is no compulsory order, nor a certainty that any problem can be solved in one go, many drawings will be needed to cope with errors. There may be errors of choice in attempting to render some feature before something else is mastered; errors of solution which are found to be based on wrong assumptions rather than wrong designs (e. g., on flat paper the three-dimensionality of the head must be forgotten and replaced by a device in the drawing itself, and one may assume that ears must be behind the face, so falsifying the proportions); errors in the perception of something not belonging to the face, such as light and shadow; errors in the rendition, particularly if colors are used, but even when they are not, as when one does not know whether working on the apparent defect or on something around it will remedy the impression. If we add glasses, hats, scarves, earrings and makeup to the face, we have need for more trials to take care of it all.

Some of the collections of drawings by one child show an extremely perceptive person being challenged again and again by the problems of conscious seeing. Very often that promising artist completely stops using a drawing tool or colors and joins the rank of the "un-gifted" who do nothing with their talents. Thus, we get the confirmation that for children, drawing is not for the expression of talent and the choice of future social involvement or a career, but a convenient way of making a study of oneself in a dialogue with the universe of perception.

But even future artists need this study and this dialogue.

Another phase in children's drawing appears when they attempt to analyze movement and another phase when they want to understand action.

Rather than a study of visual perception, drawings are then only opportunities to objectify the "feel" of oneself in a state of motion: walking, running, climbing, falling, bending, lifting, grasping, holding on. Which muscles are representative of each of these states: legs, back, arms, hands, the whole body? The dialogue this time is between the hand that draws and the mind that is somatically questioning parts of the soma.

Remarkable results can be reached by some of these analysts, who may lack the draftsman's know-how but not an entry into the challenge. Some schoolchildren's drawings have been praised by consummate painters for having achieved without schooling what years of study are not able to make available. The obvious explanation of this paradox is that children dwell in their activity; their consciousness inhabits their state and lets their self — which has unified everything in the bag — find the transmutations of the project that coordinate their feeling with their will and the instruments they have available. The intellect is held in check in the child but not in the adult.

Similarly one finds that other problems with which experienced artists struggle a great deal can be solved by children who do not claim to have any artistic schooling - for example, the smile on a face, or the exaggeration of some feature that forcibly conveys a definite message.

The problems of composing a picture containing multitudes of figures, such as enemy battalions meeting on a battlefield, does not seem to deter the young draftsman who gets on with his job and places his soldiers here and there, his cannon, his trenches, trees, fortifications, flags and reserves. Once the drawing is done it is abandoned as if it were soiled paper. Sartre's statement that "the artist is more precious than his work," because he can produce more works with equal ease, applies to such children and they seem to know it. Another occasion, another piece of paper, a little time, and another battle will be enacted on the space available.

These frescoes may become more realistic when the laws of perspective are taught at school. But even without perspective the spatial arrangement, the position of the various arms and the weapons, the angles of the bodies, are all testimony to a mind full of consciousness of what makes action and how to display it on any scale.

We can say about perspective that its discovery is not a necessity, and indeed it was not discovered by many civilizations which lasted for centuries. It was found and first used by Italian Renaissance painters and then taught to every aspiring artist. It has since been universally used by painters except when the cubists and other abstractionists have questioned its dominance. Children who have lived with action have ample experience that the distortions which result from a particular viewpoint are illusory, since they know that the small becomes large when we come near it and the large gets small when we are far from it. So the image can be corrected in the mind through knowledge supported by evidence.

Our eye, that we have educated for years, can be educated again at any stage and when we become acquainted with the rules of perspective we can produce images which take it into account. We use thought to give images a flexibility which makes it possible to recognize that a drawing displays a viewpoint that transforms what we have perceived rather than catalogues our perceptions in a particular order. Practice in drawing involving perspective gives us an eye that sees it in the environment as realistically as it sees colors or shapes. However, the mind transcends this modification of the image and can reach new transformations that may affect the image very differently. In particular it can conceive of counter-perspective and of mixing primitive, cubist and realistic images as a project in the mind.

The boys and girls we have been looking at through their work are not investing in the future and valuing their production but are using some available instruments to reach self-knowledge, a self-knowledge that is concerned with the analytic powers of their minds in relation to the overall synthetic power of sight. The self-knowledge is not an end in itself; it is to become yet another instrument with which to dominate the environment and to master some relationships with it.

In some societies such an education was considered necessary for coping with challenges and dangers and was seen as demanded by life and essentially biological. In modern urban societies it is only a short phase of one's life and most people do not regret not having become painters. Most people do not even suspect that they gave themselves such an education and that they hold a gift they can use to give themselves satisfaction and enjoyment.

It remains true that seeing is a mental functioning structured by reality. In animals it is conditioned by instinct but in man the education of seeing changes reality and makes hidden aspects visible. Babies and boys and girls spontaneously take upon themselves the task of giving themselves a more adequate, more penetrating, more precise, and more analytic sight, in exercises which at a certain period include drawing. The synthesis of play and drawing yields a self more in command of itself and readier to affect its own evolution.

There is room in this for further education, as we shall see later, this time occasioned by the intervention of educators who can offer new opportunities which make sense at once.

8 Partnerships

Anyone who has seen children of elementary school age change schools, or move from one area to another, has noticed with what ease the links with school friends or neighbors and constant companions are forgotten. It seems that emotional and sentimental connections are not for this age. And this is in agreement with the major stress on action.

What we shall consider most seriously as adolescents is barely a matter of attention now, for all the dialogues are with the self involved in activities mainly requiring an egocentric attitude. Skills demand concentration on the task and a reduction of any distractions. Hence, there is no real demand for anything beyond a momentary linkage to others, and only as long as this serves the end in mind. In the period preceding adolescence, and more so the further they are from it, boys and girls know how to use others for their own ends. This is not done as a deliberate exploitation of others; it is in fact a partnership where each partner uses the other.

So long as a partner is needed to achieve an investigation that the self meets and recognizes as vital, the partner is welcomed and involved as an alter ego in the investigation. The appearance is of a solid friendship based on common interest and mutual benefit as well as delight in each other. But beware! The slightest infringement by one of them on the expectations of the other causes everything to break down. The broken rule seems so much more important than the friendship that the friend of a minute ago becomes a villain with whom no intercourse is now possible. Sometimes a ritual formalizes the break; for example, two crossed fingers of one partner are separated by a finger of the other. After such rituals each will look for another partner to pursue the vital game, ready to break the new friendship if it is as unsatisfactory as the first, and so on.

Of course, since feelings are high at the time, and the reasons that generated the indignation are not very deep, a broken friendship can be and often is mended. Nevertheless, the links are essentially fragile and no one truly attempts to make them stronger. They are subordinated to the function of the partnership, which is the selfish growth of the partners engaged in the activities of the time, which unfortunately cannot be undertaken by oneself alone.

If by chance rules are not broken, and more and more games that involve more than one person are gone through to the satisfaction of the partners, a lasting friendship may result which continues through adolescence to become friendship for life. But how many of us have had them, or have even heard of them in the case of others?

8 Partnerships

Boys and girls are not yet gregarious and do not go out of their way to belong to a gang, but they know very well that for some activities and some games they have to team up with others to make the thing work. Pragmatically they form groups to play hide-and-seek, to leapfrog, to play card games, to do some acting, to be in any one of the hundreds of games where one's mastery of the activity requires competitors or associates or arbiters.

That they learn some of the time, or almost all of the time, something about the behavior of their peers or other children is obvious but incidental, and there are so many occasions where they seem not to be learning much about social intercourse that this cannot be fortuitous. Since children at this age are devoted to the study of action the social forms which are compatible with it will be entertained, will take form, take root; others will be noticed if something striking accompanies them; many will not reach consciousness clearly and will be ignored.

Insofar as it is routine, the rules of life in a family are observed and parents find this age far less demanding than earlier or later ones. So long as they are left alone to play with their ready-made toys or those they make up for themselves, they will not ask for attention. So long as they can watch their cartoons, their mystery stories, their murder stories on TV, they will be no trouble. Since they neither have opinions on matters discussed on political, economic or social levels, nor have personal needs beyond the purchase of some toys or some materials to make things for certain purposes, like a first-aid box, or decorations for a festival, they do not attempt to enter into transactions for money as they will do later.

They are, of course, ready to give up a small amount of time to chores which are not too difficult in exchange for some consideration and some peace to play their vital games. They take for granted that they belong to a family, but do not give it the blind loyalty that adolescents give even when the generation gap moves them to leave it. Generally boys and girls remain at home unless they are the victims of extremely rare conditions of antagonism, mainly because they are not yet moved to look at their home critically. Their fertile imaginations make real conditions, whether of poverty or cleanliness or tidiness, less noticeable, supplying factors which embellish the space. Rats and cockroaches, lizards and ants, are not more than nuisances.

All the qualities of mind which were needed in the past when homes were not cut off from nature are part of the equipment of boys and girls. They do not mind having to wear a torn or inelegant garment; neither do they think that overmuch washing is good for them. What matters is that they have a place, a social place where they can do what they want to do. Society is all right so long as it leaves them alone and does not ask them to do much more than take care of themselves on their own terms.

On the one hand they show great indifference towards what is transcendental and, on the other, extreme vulnerability to the observance of rules and rituals in games, making them intolerant, vindictive, and even cruel.

This description of boys and girls bears considerable resemblance to certain adult societies where most members of the group have a sensitivity to what touches their interest coupled with a total indifference to what concerns others, making so many evil group behaviors possible.

In the case of elementary school boys and girls they do not question the fact that they belong to this family, this community, this state and this country. It is part of the given that they have no desire to change. There is enough for them to do to know the environment as a fact, even perhaps an eternal fact, that may have been there from the beginning of the world — that is, with their coming into it.

Indeed, how can one want to change one's environment if one does not yet know it or know a different one? First, then, one devotes one's time to assimilating the environment and gets a lot of fun doing it because of the expansion of oneself that goes with it. Much later, when one's mind is furnished with this and other real or imagined realities, one thinks of altering the aspects of the environment that strike one as changeable. If enthusiasm for social action can be created in boys and girls it is generally short-lived, and even then it is the content <u>per se</u> which mobilizes them. Cleaning one's street can be fun, once, if many people get involved, if things are visibly moved. But cleaning one's street every day is of no interest to them because it has no meaning in the vital work they require to do for themselves.

Permanent groupings beyond the family do not attract them and if they are formed in a street or a building the reasons for staying together escape them and are capable of breaking down at the slightest provocation. Brothers or sisters, cousins and neighbors, fight with each other all the time, not through malice or hatred nor even dislike, but because each is an opportunity for the other to know himself as a teaser, a victim, a more skilled fighter, capable of obtaining favors from others, of being protected by others, of exploring the harmlessness of some acts and the dangers of others. Brothers and sisters so often give the impression of being enemies, ready to jump at each other's throat, threatening each other with eternal disowning, but returning soon afterwards to exploit each other in a game both want to play and cannot play without the other.

Boys and girls who are so knowledgeable in the field of action pay the price of being deprived of criteria in the fields where their elders are consciously living. They therefore have to guess much of the meaning of social intercourse and are more often wrong than right in their guesses.

Since they have developed a more liberal sense of property than in their first years and do not need to own static objects in order to know them as they did then, they pay far less attention to who owns what and can unthinkingly take someone else's property. This makes them delinquent in the eyes of the adults in their environment but they have no sense of guilt, as they will in later years, since there was no inner participation in the act.

Objects have functions for them as people do. They can be assimilated for their function but not per se. Just as boys and girls can drop partners for not sharing their own standards in the observance of rules, they can enter into temporary relationships with objects and not develop any attachment to them. Boys and girls can easily become vandals without any intention of wrongdoing. Since there is an action to perform, the action dictates its completion, and if this is the destruction of a piece of furniture or windows or any other object, they put their whole self in it. To outsiders they appear to be simply vandals. There were no extraneous moral issues in their minds when they engaged in the action; there cannot be after the event.

Adults are baffled by the thoroughness of the destruction; children are baffled by the reference to elements such as cost, public ownership or ugliness, which are transcendental and hence invisible. When Rousseau suggested teaching Emile the consequences of breaking windows by letting him catch a cold, he was telling us not only that lessons at the level of direct perception are right for children of that age but also that he did not have a very good solution for vandalism. Indeed, pneumonia and death are not equivalent to a pane of glass. Nevertheless, one of the most influential thinkers in education could not understand that boys and girls, like all of us, live at their own level of awareness and must be met there. No one can insert into a boy's consciousness that some actions which do not present any danger to him are reprehensible, or that he should stick to his partners even when these do not seem to perform their function in the partnership.

The questions this raises are more matters of education than of epistemology and we want to keep them separate for the sake of study. Only when we are really in contact with the workings of the mind of boys and girls will there be any chance that valid educational suggestions will be forthcoming.

In this chapter we have tried to understand why the involvement in action permits only some aspects of life to reach the mind and blocks others, and we have met the constant factor of awareness, which is always awareness of something definite until awareness of one's awareness becomes one's lot. This development, on the whole, does not happen before mid-adolescence and, even if it happens, it does not seem to remain with everyone.

There are so many jobs asking for the total attention of the children we are looking at that we must not be surprised that many others are neglected and escape awareness. They are not protected from, or even warned about, these matters and in them lie the dangers of misunderstanding between members of the same group of different ages.

If children do not understand adults the converse is also true.

9 Equity, Morality

In our study of boys and girls we have opportunities to study mankind when we come to fundamental questions such as the psychological foundations of morality. Because several generations live simultaneously on Earth there seems to be a movement of knowledge (of any kind) from the older generations to the younger ones. However, in most fields we must learn from scratch, all of us, and prepare ourselves to take responsibility for our actions. The experience of others serves us little, and when it does it is in specific ways for which we also need preparation. Morality is no exception.

If, indeed, babies find organized environments around them and if they are neither equipped <u>in utero</u> for these environments to affect them completely at once, nor spontaneously interested in some of their aspects, we find them accepting what they meet with equanimity and adjusting to it ungrudgingly. This, in fact, is true for all ages and generations since omniscience and omnipotence are not of this world.

Slowly guided by our self-interest, new kinds of questions emerge in each of us for which we passionately seek answers and only then learn to objectify new attitudes and thoughts which sometimes resemble those of our elders. When this happens it appears as if to grow is to adopt the mores of the environment according to a pattern that investigators can find and describe.

For the person who is absorbed in the study of some vital component in life, anything that is related to this component is accessible at once, as well as the elements referring to the mastered past. Relevance comes from the capacity of awareness to dwell in what is met. Children who are involved in an activity therefore develop at the same time a capacity to assess the world as a respondent to their needs with respect to what is involved in that activity. Within that frame of reference two distorting factors appear: one that makes us ignore much that is connected with what we are involved in, but we do not see how, and one that makes us exalt the relevance of what we see to the perceived situation.

Since what we do not perceive does not touch us we almost never move in advance to prevent ills or evils from suddenly falling on us. Our ethical mechanisms, like our sensory ones, are moved by impacts. Hence, we cannot be surprised to find boys and girls operating morally in a manner that is subordinated to their perception of themselves in the world. As mentioned in the previous chapter the consequences of their actions often seem to them entirely out of proportion since there was no other intention when they engaged in them than to perform those actions. The powers of society do not "react" to children's actions in the sense this word has in physics — where reactions are the opposite of actions — they seem to take initiatives that are unrelated to the action and to endow the actor with elements that he knows are non-existent.

Indignation is a feeling that each of us knows almost from the beginning of life and that operates automatically in most of us as a "reaction" when we perceive that we are not being equitably taken into account. While indignation is a behavior, the perception of inequity is a movement of the self that can reach certainty that what belonged to the situation has been violated and should be acknowledged as a violation by the other party.

Pulling food on which he is still feeding out of a baby's reach generates indignation which only subsides when the source is returned and the function is restored. Confiscating toys from school children likewise creates indignation. The difference between the two ages in the handling of indignation is that older children can continue to entertain it by re-evoking the circumstances, while babies abandon it completely. Equity is a judgment of the individual whose makeup and experience tells him that the circumstances demand that the people involved respect its obvious components. It is equitable for mom to give more food to dad than to the younger children. If she gives one only a little of what one dislikes, that is also equitable, but asking for the disliked food to be eaten is a trespass and generates indignation. If she gives more of what one likes to another sibling it is iniquitous and calls for indignation. What the aggrieved child calls obvious in these situations is synonymous with what he perceives even when this is invisible to everybody but himself.

On the basis of this changing ground, boys and girls live in a perfectly stable world. So long as they are guided by their perception that what is compatible with the needs of their vital functionings must be offered to them, they cannot perceive contradictions in their demands. They at once know how to turn an argument so that it looks like a perfect justification for their stand. "He started it," is one of them; "She took one more than I did," is another; "I warned you," is a third, "I tasted it and I don't like it," is one more.

Children don't have to dwell at length on moral issues for they live in the moment and their consciousness remains with the present situation. They therefore develop the tools which function in their own interest and cope with the intrusions of others while their own perception knows how to benefit from the opportunities that others present them. Both have to be available to carry on the job of living among others and of performing one's own tasks.

In the conflicts between their hardened selfish egos children learn not so much to compromise but to find out how and when they can get all of "it" or must leave some for others. Their idea of what is equitable gains flexibility and they become aware that it is advantageous to yield here and there in order to serve their self-interest better. But life does not demand of them that the responses to pinpointed challenges become principles, or that an overall view of men's motives and their behavior must be found. On the contrary they demonstrate a very remote and abstract interest in regulating the world.

9 Equity, Morality

Anyone who has attempted to give children a role in school or camp government knows that in the constitutional assembly that is empowered to formulate the rules and regulations children are perfectionists. They want the most rigid organization framed with stiff punishments for any breach of the laws, as if these could only apply to others. This abstract exercise is done with all seriousness but without much realism. It proves that they are endowed as intellects with all that is needed to link cause and effect, to respect internal coherence and acknowledge premises. It also proves that, as people, they leave the ground of experience and reality to endow their ideas with form but not content, in agreement with what they can so easily do virtually.

When they find their laws restrictive and oppressive, they walk out of them as they do from their games. But they feel neither guilty nor rebellious. They are using the logic of action and if they can get away from the grip of their promises it is a sign that the logic of action has been fulfilled. They have not yet developed loyalty to abstract coherent systems, and life commands them to break the restrictions on their actions. Actions are the higher court which passes ultimate judgment on what is sensible and acceptable and what must be rejected as unconstitutional.

There are issues for which their present awarenesses are sufficient to produce ethical behaviors that can be justified by the whole self. There are others which can confuse a child but where he has some entry and can sort them out after experimentation and reflection, and there are issues where he has neither entry nor interest and, for these, utter confusion and even despair are the only adequate forms of response.

Because of this structuration of the world of ethics there are always issues that are controversial and form the ground on which moral education thrives. It is sufficient to put a question slightly beyond what one has investigated to find that answers are inconclusive or even definitely of the type, "I do not know." The so-called stages of moral development are a solidification of a fluid situation in which consciousness must be struck by a challenge — which must therefore be of a nature that can be comprehended by the self-engaged in exploring a part of the total universe, and hence be accessible to its present intelligence and its spontaneous functionings. That morality develops on parallel tracks to cognition is an obvious, even if superficial, observation. It is obvious because we develop as a person on many fronts and our cognitive development will be reflected in our moral growth, and conversely. S is superficial because both developments are manifestations of total growth, which can only be of awareness of the self engaged in making itself for its own ends and not attempts to reach a level represented by someone else's growth.

Looking at awareness at work — in its dual movement of making the self that produces the objectivations that are compatible with the external energy inputs and the inner dynamics, and the employment of these objectifications to cope with wider chunks of the universe — we find that there is a time to go through the awareness of action, producing a logic of action and a morality of action for, among other things, the purpose of making the self into a master of that aspect of the universe. When this job is done the new challenges that can now be met will bring another upsurge of the self that will find another universe to conquer, to structure, to become familiar with; and with new cognitive instruments a new morality will show itself.

The stress on conscious living which guides us in our studies requires that we look at morality as one of the aspects of living, an aspect that tells us as much about the evolution of awareness as any other. So long as the self is seeing that part of the universe that can be seen with the polarized awareness that comes from immersion in action, we shall find traces of that immersion in all its manifestations.

If boys and girls are working to conquer all that is conquerable in their environment through the instruments of awareness of action, interpersonal problems will gain certain features from this awareness. Their involvement in them will depend on, and will be conditioned by, what is accessible to that awareness. To the extent that every person is complete at every moment, the ethical awareness or the intellect or the affectivity that is manifested at that time will be all one has to go by. Hence, rather than consider that one stage is lacking something that will be completed in the behavior of another stage, we can look at what anyone can do with given equipment operating within a certain awareness.

A preconception often associated with the word "development" makes us look at what we have only in relation to what we lack as compared to someone else who has it, and development then seems to require that we rush through the transient to reach the permanent. If evolution is an attribute of man, perhaps only transient stages are possible and permanence may be an attribute of something that cannot evolve any more. Techniques that study the transformation of viewpoints, that renew the manifestations of the self because the self sees new universes to be explored and engages in them, may be required for a brief grasp of what one is and what one is becoming.

The evolution of morality, no less than the evolution of other aspects of the self, will be better grasped if we acknowledge that as people who animate our world through our participation, we shall manifest an ethic that agrees with our enlightenment, rather than one that lacks some features which may develop if we live long enough in a particular social environment.

As moral beings we generate ethics. The concomitant existence of many people impinging on each other to obtain personal fulfillment and benefit creates the problems of relativity and conflict. Relativity gives everybody equal rights to think and feel as they do, but most observers give themselves the right to represent the apex, or at least the average level, of morality. From this results the conflicts that embroil those who think or feel differently but demand to be equally accepted as guides of society.

Even though it ascertains that man is a moral being, this competition between would-be guides says that man still has to grow enough to be able to take the relativity of moral perceptions as a fact and give himself a functional model acceptable to everybody.

9 Equity, Morality

Empirically we all live next to each other, some of us more capable than others of putting up with pressures and rationalizing the behaviors of those who at the same time say they love us and only want us to be different from what we are. Empirically we manage on the whole to survive mainly because the resilience of the self finds spaces, and even universes, where we are left alone because no one around seems interested in dwelling in them.

Boys and girls, much more than adolescents and adults, prove this resilience by being impervious to moral teaching and only taking on some of the forms in order to get adults off their backs. By engulfing themselves in actions capable of cutting them off from the rest of the world, they find activities, day after day, that no longer interest adults, that look harmless, and are perfect vehicles for their dual purpose of being themselves and not being influenced by others.

Boys and girls are moral beings who own an ethic that guides their actions when other people are involved, but which is of little account when they are on their own. When they look at themselves in the world they know that what is most important is their vital education and the ethic that tells them to give it their greatest attention, for from their activities a whole person will emerge with criteria and sure sight, a person one can count on, who knows how to live in the universe of action with confidence and equanimity.

That such a confident person looks with a kind of indifference on the sermons which parents shower on him should not surprise us. Many of the adult's words are still empty of meaning and are so passionately delivered that confusion results, although it is not necessarily perceived as one's own confusion. Perhaps, the child may think, it is the state of one who does not know as well as I do that the facts speak for themselves.

The fullness of life that boys and girls enjoy serves as a much more reliable testimony that they are right in their ethical behaviors than the endlessly repeated "should"s and "don't"s uttered by their elders, which do not seem to apply to the behaviors as they are known from inside. That wrong, and even harm or evil, may result from actions will become understandable to the expert in action that each elementary school child is when he is confronted with a genuine situation where actions and not words are the vehicle for comprehension.

There is a lesson for educators to learn here. In a subsequent publication we shall attempt to consider this point.

10 Interest and Lack of Interest

It is an old adage among elementary school teachers that boys and girls reach their schools keen and enthusiastic and that two years later many of them have dropped out and are only present in body. Many teachers all over the world are at a loss to provide children of this age with meaningful activities. It is no wonder then that such innovative proposals as open education, the Nuffield Mathematics Project, the EDC science project, and so on, have been produced to rescue students in schools.

These and other projects suggest that as long as students have some activity to absorb they will enjoy school, and from these activities they will gain some academic knowledge valued by adults. This guiding principle confirms that observers have noted the dedication of children to action and have wanted both to nourish it and to use it in their manipulation of school children to make them cover a certain curriculum.

Since boys like to fiddle with anything electrical, a kit can be given them which asks them to use the items and lets them know they have done it correctly when a bell rings.

Since boys and girls like to play with water, with sand, with clay, there must be corners in the school, or even each classroom, where children can find these materials and play with them.

Since boys and girls enjoy making noises, a separate space should be provided where they can beat drums or cymbals or other percussion instruments.

Since they like to paint, there should be easels and paints and freedom to use them in another space to produce their pictures. Since they like to draw, desks should be provided which will also be useful for those who discover writing and enjoy it.

The whole organization is visibly made to subordinate school activities to the spontaneous interests shown by students and noted by their teachers. A great step has been taken by those who now offer an education based on children's interests. Another great step is being taken by those who offer children an education that does not require that they use themselves as adults do. This education is inspired by the analysis of the development of the cognitive powers of children exemplified in Piaget's work.

So many educators are at the present time fascinated by these two approaches, based respectively on the interests and on the lack of interests in children, that we must devote at least a few pages to these subjects.

In order to conclude that the earth is round it is not enough to look at the horizon or at the rising sun, or to know the fact that circumnavigation is possible. We need to have <u>a priori</u> an integrative schema in our mind that will reconcile all these experiences, that call on different criteria for each experience. For millennia the sun rising in the East and setting in the West could be observed as a daily fact of experience. It carried with it the notion that the sun traveled the sky to turn around the earth, as the appearance supported. But when an alternative schema was suggested which could more adequately reflect a number of isolated facts, each calling for a special theory, it served to start a true mental revolution that still affects us.

All this tells us that an accumulation of 'correct' observations cannot compete victoriously with an insight that gives these observations a deeper meaning while opening new fields of investigation. Copernicus made the work of Kepler and Newton and thousands of lesser astronomers, physicists and mathematicians possible. We still talk of a Copernican revolution when a single idea starts people off on a new track, that respects all the known facts while illuminating them differently, and only requests the abandonment of a traditional idea.

Children's interest is only a symptom of a deeper involvement. <u>Inter est</u> (which means: to be inside, to be with it) would be a more precise description of involvement. To find what holds children's attention we need to find the springs of growth. Many people believe that growth takes place because time passes, as if the rotation of the earth could cause the actual experiences we go through. For many others growth is inscribed in the molecules that form DNA. For some, among whom I count myself, all growth in man is growth of awareness even when it is also biological growth. The passage of time is marked by its change into experience. Time as a notion is itself an awareness.

In the temporal hierarchies which form the structuration of experience we find the most fruitful instrument that can be offered to psychologists and epistemologists for the understanding of the concreteness of individual growth. In "The Universe of Babies" I have already shown how much more accessible the functioning of babies and the reasons for the order of their actual appearances become when awareness is the light. Interests can also be much better understood when they make their appearance.

The age-old awareness that time is an awareness in which a past, a present and a future can be separated applies to each instant as well as to the life of any individual or of any group of men. If the slicing of time is simultaneously applied to an individual and a group it appears that what remains to be lived by the individual includes what has already been lived by many other members of the same group: that there are experiences to come whose nature is known to others, even if the concrete content is not known to them and can only be known existentially by the individual who lives it.

In what is the future today for an individual — it will become his past one day — there are inaccessible features. Nevertheless, that future is immanent for him since it is present in the group. For the individual the features of the transcendental are inaccessible, but since he lives among people who have actualized some of its content he can perceive the actual that has a form at his level, even if most of what goes with it escapes him completely.

The model becomes more complex, but also more precise and more useful, if we place at intermediate stages those people who are at different moments in their actualization of the content.

The "law of spiritual contagion" which links the growths of people at various stages of their experience tells us that an individual is inspired to devote himself to some activity if he has access to it but has not yet explored it. Contagion requires spiritual, experiential, proximity. Contagion is the spring which throws children into games that they do not know, but that other children are playing at a level too advanced for them to make sense of it with what they have done with themselves so far. Contagion maintains the shifts to other levels of activity in conjunction with the awareness that time is being changed into experience and the awareness that the self is integrating the new by recasting the old into it.

Because of these dynamics it is safer to say that the descent of the future shapes our life rather than that the past pushes us ahead.

The last statement gives to the unknown the power to change our lives and rejects the current view that to reach the unknown we have to change it into the known.

Children are moved to be interested in exactly the same way as adults. The difference lies in what will mobilize the self in each.

For boys and girls of elementary school age it is the universe of action; for adults today it may be social and political matters, economic or environmental advantages. Everyone, whatever his age, has to become more himself in order to gather the fruits of his dedication to what matters most to him. Boys and girls show an interest in what is accessible in the immanent and a lack of interest in the inaccessible transcendental. So do adults.

In proposing that activity <u>per se</u> may be motivating for elementary school children we neglect the direction of the overall growth of each child. In proposing a translation of our presentations into terms that agree with the Piagetian description of this age, we impose a ceiling where there should be an inspiration to move towards what is to come. Both proposals seem to miss the dynamics of growth and the fact that the co-presence of individuals at different stages in their evolution is capable of creating a contagion which, in cooperation with the unknown, helps each to become more himself.

The study of games in streets and playgrounds clearly indicates that growth is directed by the temporal hierarchies generated by the simultaneous presence of definite tasks and of people around who are at various stations on their way to mastery. While we must be moved from inside in order to perform, and therefore relate what we do to what we have already done, we can only find an entry into what we have not yet done if we perceive that someone in front of us is doing it (except in those few cases when we plunge into a task because it conveys to us that it is possible).

Once we have found a way in, our interest at once feeds back to us whether we should remain or quit. Hence, educators can use interest as an external indicator that the task is proper for that age and stage, but cannot say that if we turn our back on the task we lack interest in it. The conclusion can only be that we have either not found an entry into it or that no one has offered us a way in.

The Piagetian educators, instead of being creative and breaking through barriers, have made these barriers impregnable, surrounded by an impassable precipice. No doubt the presentation of activities to children of this age, because it coincides with what their consciousness dwells in, takes to them what works, and the success that ensues blurs the issues. Traditional teaching is based on the premise that verbal transactions can replace activity, even prior to active exploration, simply because man has managed to save himself much time and energy by inventing language. This premise is only false in that it offers language before action; language then remains arbitrary since only when meanings are offered to support words can language become a vehicle of communication and words be retained. Piaget and others have called for activity to precede verbalization and put that error right, but they have let themselves stop there, not realizing that activity too can be idle if it is not integrated from within in the larger scheme of individual growths and with the help of contagion and inspiration.

It is possible, as we shall spell out in a subsequent publication, to give teachers a creative role and offer children of this age action-games which make sense at the same time as they open worlds to the self for continuous exploration. In playing these games children prove that they do not obey the law of Piaget's stages, that they can use their inner dynamics to let the future restructure their mind and start a different adventure from that of their ancestors.

Temporal hierarchies are compatible with the integrative functions of the self, as they have shown from the time of the self's conception, and they can present new sequences-of-being, provided they respect the demands of the objectified parts of the self and the true dynamics of its energy. There will still be growth through the four states of learning in each acquisition of skills; there will still be room for the multiplicity of experiencing in one and the same group. But now, instead of only showing respect for the individual, we can show respect for the reality of the co-existence of people at different stages in their growth that produces levers for the advance of everyone on the road to knowing themselves as learning systems engaged in particular dialogues with their inner and outer universes.

If children clearly stratify the world so that some aspects of it evoke their interest while others leave them indifferent, and if we know how to provide means that displace the boundaries, we do not eliminate the structure that time gives to the universe. We leave intact the fact that (for each of us) some things are transcendental at all stages and levels. The presence of the transcendental is the ultimate lever of growth for all of us taken together. It has so many forms in so many cultures and civilizations, arrived at by those who were struck by the mystery of mankind's complexity and dynamics, by the co-presence of appearance and reality, by the inability to absorb more than a portion of the majestic whole, that many individuals are made to sense their shortcomings rather than their advantages. For boys and girls the transcendental is not yet experienced as the depth that contains so much. They neither feel dwarfed, as so many adults do, nor do they attempt to do more than grow within the layers immediately above them. So they look sure of themselves, get mobilized fully and at once, remain undistracted by social and even natural upheavals.

During a war they can be caught by the excitement of not being in their bedrooms and spending nights in the shelters, almost unaware of danger, interested in the sirens more than in enemy fire. When they read adventures involving people fighting, they accept the author's reasons for siding with one or the other of the opposing parties and make no personal judgment of who is entitled to sympathy. What moves them is the involvement in a battle, a struggle, a turmoil, as we can see when we are in a movie theater or in front of the television; all our muscles are excited by the scenes and we participate with the fighters by giving or receiving punches virtually. This virtual participation accounts for the excitement of the audience at football and boxing matches.

Villains may be people as much as the heroes, but only the heroes generate sympathy. However terrible the enemy's lot, simply because it is the enemy all source of understanding is lacking and the most cursory dismissal of its case is accepted. The involvement of readers in an account of a massacre can be so one sided that it seems to be equivalent to the absence of any moral fiber. A state of mind, which may be acceptable in the case of boys and girls, can last through the totality of one's life if it is not shaken off during adolescence. The transcendental contains action as well as love and charity, but only action inspires children, and those who are the protagonists of action are admired provided they do not carry the opprobrium of the environment. The workings of these brakes on inspiration tell us that beyond the layer of objectifications of action there are other layers, invisible and transcendental now, but known as immanent since they affect the consciousness. In this case they affect us by not letting us admire action irrespective of who performs it.

Throughout history rulers, as long as they occupied the seat of power, have received applause from most of their subjects for their actions, whatever they were. But once-worshipped heroes can easily turn into villains — and many did. Their lot was then no better than that of their enemies.

As boys and girls grow, many of their springs can be activated by new elements from the immanent, and some of their interests change as these elements descend into their lives. The stress shifts without destroying the past and the involvements generate new appearances. What seems to be the center of one's inner life is now on the way to becoming inner layers that will be covered by more layers as time goes by. The past becomes less operative, and from outside, too, the appearances show that one has changed, has grown out of certain forms.

Interest may shift, first within a layer of the self, and later from one layer to a surrounding one. Successive interests look similar when consciousness remains within one layer but can look very different when an interest resides in one layer and another in the next. As seen from within one layer, interests are determined, together with a lack of interest in what is in the next. As seen when shifting from one layer to the next, consciousness slowly sheds its involvement in one kind of activity while timidly attempting to take on another.

Almost without noticing, the appeal of the activities in one layer is reduced when mastery of what was challenging in it is achieved, and without much excitement one finds oneself pulled to try something new. Excitement increases as soon as one finds some stepping-stones in the new activities and it is evident that one has shifted interest when one is absorbed by the new.

The old is, of course, still available and if need be one can pick up any challenge in that layer and show ease in handling it. But this ease is not equivalent to the profound involvement which was apparent when the self was seeking to integrate what was being lived. Enjoyment can be obviously present, but nevertheless the quality of the presence of the self in the activity, to the self at least, is certainly not that of a seeker, of a keen person attempting to prove something to himself. Perhaps it is being done only to verify that one is still on top.

Observers who have consciousness of these functionings can see that there are two kinds of lack of interest just as there are two kinds of interests. Both can be described in terms of the presence or absence of awareness. For the master the easy tasks are not appealing simply because they no longer challenge and look to him like chores. They can be done, and are done if one has a reason, but excitement will be absent or superficial. For the same person the transcendental, at that stage, may find no channel to reach the self and stimulate it.

In both cases the lack of "interest" can be visible.

But when one is stimulated, attracted, challenged, the "interest" simply says precisely that. Its display is the symptom for the involvement of the self, it manifests the desire to prove to oneself that one can be equal to the challenge. The inescapable call or pull on the self is producing an interest that only proves that one is "with it;" the less compelling demand to prove to oneself that one can be on top of a challenge, because this stretches over a longer period for most vital activities, is concerned with the kind of interest we hyphenated. "In it" and "with it" are expressions that may emphasize this subtle difference. By the first we can indicate a loss of the self through involvement; by the second, that awareness is in control, is capable of detachment while not losing contact with what matters.

We need a more articulated way of dealing with such discriminations that are not less real for being subtle. Until observers become interested in the study of interest we shall only have broad encounters with what demands both a synthetic perception and pinpointed precision in the description. An attempt has been made in this chapter to indicate the value of such an approach.

11 Before Adolescence

In the previous chapters we lumped together five years of our lives and only made explicit distinctions in terms of the activity we were studying, assimilating change in age to the shift from contact with it to mastery of it. This was the functional meaning of the age that needed stressing.

While boys and girls will soon shoot up and gain in volume, in weight, and in a greater storage for energy, they have during those years controlled their growth to permit them, on the whole, to work on the fine functionings of the soma as it engages in the various actions that man has been able to devise over the generations.

Each successive year of life is obviously a smaller fraction of the whole of one's life already lived. Each year is relatively more important when we are young than when we are old and gives our past a greater weight in all we contemplate as we grow older.

Hence, as we approach adolescence — which for me is the period of our life when we devote ourselves to the study of our inner dynamics, to affectivity — our interests will show some shifts that are not visible at the beginning of the period we are studying in this book. In this chapter we shall concentrate on the announcement of the arrival of adolescence and what it does to boys and girls.

The universe of action does not close down at adolescence and adult life is filled with it. Sports, games, TV shows, all prove that it remains part of life, but the involvement of consciousness differs radically. For boys and girls it is the fabric of the universe; afterwards it becomes the support for designs and materials that fill it with something else.

We occasionally saw in previous chapters that some games that have a temporary attraction are coupled with some other activity. A player of marbles can buy, sell, or exchange marbles. This has nothing to do with the game but is a way of seizing an opportunity offered by the social framework available to the players. Another example is the opportunity to try oneself in the role of a leader or a follower in games which involve competing teams that are formed anew every time people meet to play.

Most games have a background of other people and social intercourse and offer opportunities to engage in something besides the main definition and purpose of the games. Adults may stress monetary gain or prestige or the chance to meet influential people, etc., when they take up card games, or a professional status when involved in national or international games (some of the latter serving political ends).

For most boys and girls these opportunities are less perceptible and less attractive even though from time to time someone draws their attention to the advantage of stressing the discovered opportunity and pursuing it systematically to a notable success in adulthood. Very few boys and girls, for instance, see practicing a musical instrument as an action that might make them concert artists if they pursue it, even when they feel attracted to exploring the possibilities of making sounds with a, certain know-how. Very few boys and girls become celebrated acrobats although almost all are fascinated by the exercises and attempt to enter them. They do not know their present flexibility as a wealth to preserve, only as a gift to use for self-knowledge. And it seems that self-knowledge is a shade different from the exploration of all that one can do with oneself.

Indeed, self-knowledge appears more constantly as a motivation of man's functioning than any other, for it would otherwise be difficult to understand the simultaneous possibility of total involvement in, and of dropping out of, the same activity. It is also self-knowledge that acknowledges the appearance in one's life of a new universe with a kind of command from above that one must explore it.

If boys and girls appear cruel to observers when they submit some animals to torture, in order to know if they can remain indifferent in the presence of other people's misfortunes, if they hold no grudge over temporary mistreatment or beatings, and if they fight savagely and soon afterwards act as friends to their opponents, all this tells us that children of this age have only a marginal entry into the world of feeling that will become their main concern in adolescence. The stress being on action, feelings are less compelling. As action reaches the boundaries required by the present circumstances and opportunities it, too, will become less compelling and the self freed to engage in another universe.

No doubt there is always a certain amount of contact with feeling before adolescence. The self indeed creates its sensitivities and perceives what is forced upon it. But the key involvement is in the subordination of all that comes from life to the main requirement of life that the self link itself functionally to the outer world by creating all the instruments that lead to its domination. Social elements are judged favorably or unfavorably according to whether they cooperate with one's project or not. A divorce in the family can be more or less traumatic according to whether it reduces or enhances one's chance of pursuing one's own life. A removal to another town likewise. Social events are not seen as social, with their own particular dynamics; they are nuisances, or not much of anything, unless they affect one's life — through reflection or the cultivation of existing sensitivities — drawing one to social reform against one's spontaneous interests.

We can therefore look at both sides of the boundary of adolescence and define the areas before and after the threshold: the first is the one in which the need to know the world of action is still predominant, perhaps with hints that feelings are winking at the self and encouraging flirtation with them; the second is the one in which the world of action is less dominant and feelings definitely solicit one's awareness.

"Less dominant" does not mean more than it says: still dominant, but leaving room for other involvements that can encroach on it, while this was unthinkable, not even permitted, earlier.

Action seems to stress the outside world, but in fact it cannot exist without the self and its inner workings. So we are concerned here with inner shifts, inner dynamics, movements of awareness. Stressing action is the climate of the early years of the age we are looking at; stressing the awareness that the universe of action, as one has become involved in it, has yielded most of what can be perceived and has led to a satisfactory education in terms of finesse, range and variety, is the climate of the latter years. These climates contain the criteria for the self to decide on a move — at least tentatively — while the routine activities continue. Only through the self opening up to other impacts can the shift be realized. Since the self is always in command, for most of us, particularly in the areas just mastered and in the use of automated functionings, only the self can take the initiative in the moves. Being aware of one's awareness engaged in activity, rather than aware of one's functionings in that activity, will produce the threshold, the color and tone of the two areas about that threshold, and will command the move of attention from 100% absorption in one area to less in that and some in another.

Time becomes colored too. One knows oneself to be attracted by the new and, for a while from now on, all experiencing will be distinguishable by the presence of the shift in awareness. The threshold, as an experience, can be given a date because of the change in the relationship with time. Instead of being the flow of events and their aftermaths, time is now studded with one's noticing oneself engaged in events and their sequels. If there was no self vigilantly orchestrating experience and sifting the significance of happenings there could be no memory, no individual memory, no recall or retention; yet these belong to man-in-the-world. It is the self which, closely watching how time is changed into experience, announces at all stages whether one has done the required job to the required quality, and then either orders a continuation of the involvement or gives one the right to leave the activity to enter another that one can explore from this level of competence. It is the same self that knows what is past and what is transcendental; its functionings are identical with those of the sense of truth so that the self never deceives itself. Later, in adolescence and later still, when the ego is firmly formed and the psyche gains a kind of usurped autonomy, one's self and one's sense of truth can be violated and the individual traumatized and diminished.

As soon as it catches a glimpse of an unexplored universe the self, using intuition as its way of knowing the immanent, can command the awareness of what will be. It mobilizes all that it is and all that it has to let the unknown reshape its inner life and, subsidiarily, the outer life which carries the appearances on behalf of the real life within.

Outsiders, parents, teachers, relatives and observers, who can only reach the appearances, have to guess what the subject is doing with himself. They can only do so if they have maintained their own entry into their own dynamics so that reality is given the place that is compatible with the appearances.

Boys and girls have to be seen as moving on their own towards goals that are dictated by the self in terms of what is now vital for the pursuit of life; they now notice that action which once contained all possibilities can be felt to lack some. The breach is at the same time an assessment that a light from beyond action has reached them, and a feeling of satisfaction that they have done most of what was possible to themselves in the prevailing circumstances. Feelings and emotions of all kinds have been experienced from the time of birth or a little after, but they rarely became the center of the self's preoccupation. They were gladly put aside if they prevented the continuation of the exploration of actions. Since the latter has reached a level of satisfaction and feelings continue to be available, the self can pay attention to them. Rather than let them take second place it can entertain them, enhance them by its presence, and find that they have a reality of their own that deserves study.

Emotions are existential phenomena. They represent momentary coagulations of energy that cope with a perception (of an inner or an outer movement) and maintain the self in contact with it. They can be dissolved when the contact is no longer necessary and the energy recuperated for future use. The departing energy leaves a track in the brain that corresponds to a quality or an attribute of it, resembling a tension or a difference of potential, recognizable _per se_ beyond the quantity which it accompanied. It is the quality of the emotion persisting after the emotion itself is dissolved that permits the self to classify emotions and to form a new category of components in the functionings of the self that we call feelings.

When feelings are left unenergized they are potentially available, like all other mental material in the bag, and can be triggered like any evocation, instantly, because of all the dynamics formed over the years. When they are energized they become emotions, borrowing from the brain the difference of potential and from the residual energy available in the soma the needed amount. While the energy fuels the action the feeling maintains the nature of the action, and we see again the brain acting as a fine instrument educated for cybernetic tasks. It is unnecessary for the brain to store all the energy in itself (which in fact is everywhere in the soma) when a much more subtle operation can be managed better and faster by moving minute amounts of energy which trigger into action the many many elements that have been endowed with connections to all parts of the soma. As soon as the self recognizes certain attributes in a perception it lets them communicate with educated cells within the intricacies of the brain, triggering the feeling as well as the trained activity which will best cope with the acknowledged attributes in the perception. It releases reserves of energy as well.

All this work has been routine throughout one's life, since one must be involved in perception and action to know the outside world and read its vagaries. It remains at the disposal of the self through the educated brain that has learned, for example, to read danger in components of the environment which could have appeared harmless to perception. The complexity of the content of one's perception becomes explicit as one grows, and appreciation of some components leads to special awarenesses being given the right to permanence, to stay and guide future perceptions and actions. This is what I call the education of the brain. All cerebral functionings that are activated by the presence of the self give the brain a continuous association with the self that produces the uniqueness of the individual's responses. Only the most rudimentary responses are reflex acts that do not appear to involve the self. Reflex arcs cannot account for a refusal to act reflexively. A will is only compatible with a permanent presence of the self in all functionings. Since these have been formed in time, at particular moments of one's dialogues with the inner and outer worlds, the self has been able to do the necessary job of educating the brain to perform what the self knows is required to cope "properly" with the challenges encountered.

Feelings are concomitants of perceptions and actions in the act of living and are given a specific place in the brain just as images are. Because they accompany perceptions they are associated with the ensuing images. Nightmares prove that inner dynamics alone can mobilize, as easily as impacts from the outside world, enormous amounts of energy that produce unusual emotions in the sleeper to serve special purposes of the self in contact with itself. The self in sleep may survey the education of the brain to find out whether what it knows about the meaning of what happens to the self during the day can cope with what might happen in exceptional circumstances. The dynamics of nightmares can teach us how the self handles the energy in the bag that is connected with images, and all the inner stimulation of the brain, to cope with the possible demands of life-in-relationship. The dynamics tells us, too, that feelings are more manageable than emotions and that it will be of service to the self to deal with feelings as tension rather than with energy itself in the form of emotion, just as it found it easier to deal with possible actions in the realm of the virtual.

The self involved in living through action learned to favor virtuality for its ease and accuracy; it will do the same during adolescence by deliberately shifting from emotions to feelings, by enhancing the emotions and sorting out the dynamics of feeling from them. For this to happen an <u>a priori</u> shift from action to affectivity is required. All that the self has learned will also shift. Although action and affectivity differ by perceptible components the self recognizes that virtuality is the way of working that increases yield, that speeds up spiritual growth, and makes the boy or girl move on to explore the next layer of life. Actions are less numerous and examination of what they mean to oneself more frequent, In the beginning it is still the world of action that provides the material for brooding, for affective reflection, but the total gift of oneself to action is now missing.

The vegetative system that occupied awareness in the prenatal period and immediately after birth has been ensured of all the energy it needs in the brain, of all the supervision it needs to carry out its functions automatically. In early childhood, and in the early part of the period we study in this book, the self uses and controls the middle brain, or vegetative system, by letting the neurons of the hemispheres order inputs as well as inhibitions to take place. One of these inhibitions concerns the functionings of the pituitary. This organ, half brain and half endocrine gland, maintains in particular a rate of physical growth compatible with the exploration of action. The presence of awareness in action has as one of its expressions the placing by the upper brain of inhibitors on the middle brain that translates into a reduced activity of the glandular tissues of the pituitary. The self, which is well acquainted from its early objectification of the soma with all the tissues it has made and linked together through the grid of the nervous system and the circulatory system, can reach hierarchically into any part of the soma to command an alteration, which here will take a chemical form. The release of hormones from the pituitary is contemporary with a relaxation of interest in action and a shift of interest in the vagaries of energy <u>per se</u>. Adolescence initiates puberty and physical growth to permit the intensive study of affectivity or the dynamics of energy in the bag.

Clearly, as this movement starts and the self intuits the opening up of a new world, it triggers an interest in being more and more involved in this expression of the self. Since again it can mainly take place without assistance from the outside world, a new phase in the life of the individual announces itself. Although the momentum of the previous activities continues and appearances indicate a still dominant continuity in the expressions of the self, the truth is that an irreversible trend has been launched.

Boys and girls will meet new challenges within. They will feel that they differ more from each other than they thought and begin to stress the differences instead of the similarities. They will start thinking of themselves as boys or girls and being proud of their particularities, their distinctive games and occupations. They will begin to cultivate what it means to belong to a particular sex. From being a superficial distinction sex will gain greater and greater significance, as proved by the intense amusement or embarrassment provoked by signs, drawings and the words associated with it.

Inner discoveries will find echoes in the environment and slowly make one recognize that perhaps someone else is going through the same transformations and experiencing the same resonances in the soma. Instead of looking for playmates one now looks for a friend and investigates friendship.

All this has its beginnings in the later stages of the worship of action, and for many children represents the threshold of the downward trend that will put actions in the realm of the automatic to make room for the new rules of adolescence. Two years later these rules will have made one forget that not so long ago one belonged to another religion, to a caste and brotherhood dedicated to the rites and rituals of action.

As the earth goes round, the self moves from mastery to mastery to know itself in its place in the world to the extent its gifts permit.

Boys and girls will soon know what it is to be young men and young women in front of new worlds to integrate.

www.ingramcontent.com/pod-product-compliance
Lightning Source LLC
Chambersburg PA
CBHW080549170426
43195CB00016B/2732